taste.
ONE POT

Over 100 mouth-watering recipes

igloobooks

igloobooks

Published in 2014
by Igloo Books Ltd
Cottage Farm
Sywell
NN6 0BJ
www.igloobooks.com

SHE001 1213
2 4 6 8 10 9 7 5 3
ISBN: 978-0-85734-885-2

Food photography and recipe development: Stockfood, The Food Image Agency
Front and back cover images © Stockfood, The Food Image Agency

Printed and manufactured in China

contents.

introduction.

One pot cooking is one of the best ways to cook up delicious, hearty meals with ease. Most of the work and preparation is done ahead, so you'll have time to enjoy the company of your family and friends.

Not only is one pot cooking easy, it is also a great way to achieve a deeper, richer, more complex taste by cooking all of the flavours together in one pot, pan or dish!

The recipes that follow are not only mouth-watering, but deeply satisfying too and there is a great choice for vegetarians in every section. One pot cooking is used all around the world from Moroccan tagines and Thai curries, to risottos, stews and even puddings - the list goes on and on!

One of the advantages of one pot cooking is that you can often use cheaper cuts of meat, such as lamb shank, or beef brisket. The fat renders, which thickens the sauce and also leaves you with tender meat that has infused its flavour throughout the dish.

There are many different types of one pot techniques and cooking methods you can use, such as stewing, braising and pot-roasting. Stewing meat, usually with stock or wine, can be done on the stove in a lightly covered pan. But you can cook your ingredients in the oven, if you prefer - just roughly double the cooking times.

There are, of course, many dishes that don't involve meat, such as sweet and sour tofu, or stuffed aubergines, as well as fish dishes including baked sea bream and mustard-infused salmon. There are also plenty of soups and stews – the ultimate superfood, packed full of goodness and so simple to make in just one pot.

Here are some helpful tips:

When simmering a soup or stew, do so over a low heat so that the liquid bubbles gently around the ingredients. If you cook constantly on a high heat, the fat will emulsify and you may end up with a greasy sauce.

When adding alcohol to a pot, make sure you bring the mixture to boiling point for a few minutes, so that the alcohol evaporates, as you need to burn off the bitterness of the alcohol content.

Don't over-season your pot: if you are cooking something for a long time, the cooking liquid is reduced and concentrates a sauce, which can make your food too salty if you season too heavily at the beginning. It is better to taste your food and add seasoning at the end, if desired.

Cooking with the correct pans for the recipe will yeild the best results, however if you do not have some of the more specialised items, such as a tagine, or a paella dish, don't worry, you can use a large saucepan, or a wok.

When cooking with meat, first brown the meat in the pot you will be using – this will release the juices, caramelize, and add a deep colour to the meat. Don't trim away all of the fat before cooking. The fat with contribute to the flavour of the dish and any excess can be removed at the end.

The one pot cooking method lends itself to making large batches that can be reheated. This is not only cost-effective, but is also great for feeding large families, or planning your weekly shop. If you are concerned about the excess fat in your dishes, you can let your dish cool and spoon off any fat that has solidifies on top of the dish.

The wide range of exciting recipes that follow are arranged in easy chapters on healthy meals, super soups, winter warmers, hot 'n spicy and sweet treats. The recipes are carefully selected to ensure that they suit both novice and experienced cooks alike. Now you can create sensational dishes with minimal effort and minimal washing up!

healthy
meals.

Glass noodle salad

Prep and cook time: 25 minutes
serves: 4

Ingredients:
200 g | 7 oz glass noodles
12 green asparagus spears
45 ml | 1 ½ fl. oz vegetable oil
1 lime, juiced
1 tbsp fish sauce
1 tsp sugar
1 red chilli, sliced
2 cloves of garlic, thinly sliced
1 red pepper, sliced
1 orange pepper, sliced
1 tbsp black onion seeds

Method:
Soak the noodles in boiling water according to the packet instructions. Drain, refresh in cold water and set aside in a large bowl.

Blanch the asparagus in salted water, drain, refresh in cold water and then cut into 5 cm / 2" lengths and add to the noodles.

Mix the oil, lime juice, fish sauce, sugar, chilli and garlic together and season to taste with salt.

Mix the sliced peppers into the noodles, stir in the dressing and scatter over the black onion seeds.

Honey and lemon chicken

Prep and cook time: 40 minutes
serves: 4

Ingredients:
45 ml | 1 ½ fl. oz vegetable oil
4 chicken breasts
2 lemons, juiced
75 ml | 2 ½ fl. oz runny honey
2 tbsp chopped tarragon

Method:

Preheat the oven to 180°C (160° fan) 375F, gas 5.

Heat the oil in an ovenproof dish and brown the chicken pieces evenly on all sides and then remove it from the dish.

Mix the lemon juice, honey and 1 tablespoon of chopped tarragon together. Season with salt and pepper and pour into the dish. Lightly simmer the sauce and then place the chicken back into the dish and baste it in the sauce.

Roast in the oven for 25-30 minutes, or until it is cooked through, basting the chicken from time to time. Sprinkle the remaining tarragon on the chicken and serve with potatoes and spring greens.

Chorizo paella

Prep and cook time: 45 minutes
serves: 4

Ingredients:
45 ml | 1 ½ fl. oz olive oil
1 onion, finely chopped
2 cloves of garlic, finely chopped
225 g | 8 oz | 1 cup risotto rice
1 red pepper, diced
pinch saffron threads, dissolved in
hot water
200 g | 7 oz chorizo, sliced
750 ml | 26 fl. oz | 3 cups chicken stock
150 g | 5 oz | 1 cup frozen peas
2 tbsp chopped parsley

Method:
Heat the oil in a wide pan and gently cook the onion over a low heat until soft, but not brown. Add the garlic, cook for 1 minute then stir in the rice.

Add the chopped pepper, cook for 3 minutes then add the saffron and the chorizo. Cook until the fat starts to run from the chorizo.

Gradually pour in the stock and simmer until the stock has been absorbed and the rice is tender. Add a little more water if needed.

Add the peas, cook for 5 more minutes then season the pan with salt and pepper and stir in the parsley.

Roasted vegetables

Prep and cook time: 50 minutes
serves: 4

Ingredients:
60 ml | 2 fl. oz olive oil
8 shallots, peeled
4 carrots, peeled and quartered
2 parsnips, peeled and quartered
300 g | 11 oz pumpkin, peeled and cut into chunks
1 red chilli, finely chopped
2 tsp thyme leaves

Method:
Heat the oven to 180°C (160° fan) 375F, gas 5.

Heat the oil in a large ovenproof dish on the hob. Add the shallots, cook gently for 5 minutes then add the remaining vegetables, stir to coat them in the oil then scatter over the chilli and season with salt and pepper.

Transfer the dish to the oven and roast for 40 minutes or until the vegetables are golden brown and tender. Sprinkle the vegetables with the thyme leaves and serve.

Greek salad

Prep and cook time: 20 minutes
serves: 4

Ingredients:
1 cucumber, diced
1 green pepper, cut into strips
2 tomatoes, diced
1 red onion, sliced
1 romaine lettuce heart,
leaves torn into pieces
2 tbsp black olives
2 tbsp green olives
1 clove garlic, crushed
200 g | 7 oz | 1 ½ cups feta
cheese, diced
45 ml | 1 ½ fl. oz wine vinegar
45 ml | 1 ½ fl. oz olive oil
1 tsp capers
a pinch of sugar
2 tbsp chopped basil

Method:
Mix the cucumber, peppers, tomatoes, onion and
lettuce together.

Add the black and green olives, garlic and feta cheese.
Peel the cucumber, halve it lengthwise, scrape out the
seeds and dice the flesh.

Put the vinegar and olive oil into a jar with the capers and a
pinch of sugar and season with salt and ground black pepper.
Seal the jar and shake to mix. Toss the salad in the dressing
and serve sprinkled with the basil.

Sweet and sour tofu

Prep and cook time: 2 hours 20 minutes
serves: 4

Ingredients:
For the marinade:
60 ml | 2 fl. oz sesame oil
60 ml | 2 fl. oz dark soy sauce
60 ml | 2 fl. oz honey
3 cloves of garlic, crushed
600 g | 1 ¼ lbs tofu, cubed

For the stir-fry:
45 ml | 1 ½ fl. oz sunflower oil
4 spring onions (scallions),
finely chopped
2 cloves of garlic, finely chopped
1 red chilli, chopped
1 red pepper, chopped
1 cucumber, strips of peel
removed, chopped
1 tin of pineapple chunks, drained
45 ml | 1 ½ fl. oz dark soy sauce
30 ml | 1 fl. oz vinegar

Method:
Stir the ingredients together for the marinade in a bowl, add the tofu and mix well. Set aside for 2 hours.

For the stir-fry, heat the oil in a wok and stir-fry the spring onions, garlic and chilli. Add the pepper and cook for 5 minutes, stirring all the time.

Add the cucumber, pineapple chunks and the remaining ingredients, cook for 2 more minutes, then season with salt and pepper and serve with noodles.

Seafood mariniere

Prep and cook time: 30 minutes
serves: 4-6

Ingredients:
200 g asparagus
30 ml | 1 fl. oz olive oil
115 g | 4 oz butter
1 onion, finely sliced
5 cloves of garlic, chopped
1 red pepper, sliced
200 g | 7 oz squid rings, cleaned
100 g | 3 ½ oz baby octopus, cleaned
200 g | 7 oz white fish, cut into chunks
200 g | 7 oz king prawns,
heads removed
500 g | 18 oz mussels, cleaned
125 ml | 4 ½ fl. oz | ½ cup white wine
flat leaf parsley, chopped

Method:
Heat the oil and butter in a wide pan on a medium heat and gently cook the onion until soft, but not brown. Add the garlic and pepper, cook for 5 minutes then add the squid, baby octopus and white fish.

Cook over a high heat for 3 minutes then add the prawns, mussels and white wine.

Add the trimmed asparagus spears. Cover the dish and cook for 2 minutes or until the mussels have opened. Finally, add the chopped parsley and season with salt and pepper.

Discard any mussels that haven't opened and serve immediately with fresh crusty bread and salad.

Baked mushrooms with eggs

Prep and cook time: 20 minutes
serves: 4

Ingredients:
125 g | 4 ½ oz | 1 cup chanterelle mushrooms
125 g | 4 ½ oz | 1 cup oyster mushrooms
30 ml | 1 fl. oz olive oil
1 tbsp butter
1 tsp fennel seeds, lightly crushed
1 tsp coriander seeds, lightly crushed
4 eggs
chives, to garnish

Method:

Heat the oven to 180°C (160° fan) 375F, gas 5.

Brush the mushrooms to remove any grit and slice any large ones in half. Place the mushrooms in 4 individual ovenproof dishes and drizzle over the oil. Mix with your hands to ensure the mushrooms are thoroughly coated in the oil.

Dot the butter on top of the mushrooms and scatter over the fennel and coriander seeds. Season the dishes with salt and pepper, cover with foil and bake in the oven for 15 minutes, turning occasionally.

Boil the eggs in a pan of simmering water for about 4 minutes. Rinse under cold running water, carefully remove the shells and serve on top of the mushrooms and garnish with chives for a great snack.

Stuffed aubergines

Prep and cook time: 45 minutes
serves: 4

Ingredients:
4 large aubergines (eggplants)
60 ml | 2 fl. oz olive oil
200 g | 7 oz cherry tomatoes, halved
2 yellow peppers, chopped
75 g | 2 ½ oz fried onions, chopped
2 tbsp sultanas
180 g | 6 oz | 1 cup couscous, soaked
according to packet instructions
2 tbsp parsley, chopped
2 lemons, zest

Method:
Preheat the oven to 180°C (160° fan) 375F, gas 5.

Cut the aubergines in half lengthways and scrape out the seeds and place them in an ovenproof dish.

Mix the oil, tomatoes, peppers, onions, and sultanas with the couscous, season with salt and pepper and place into the cavities of the aubergines.

Cover the dish tightly and bake in the oven for 25-30 minutes. Scatter over the parsley and lemon zest and serve.

Tomato pasta bake

Prep and cook time: 30 minutes
serves: 4

Ingredients:
500 g | 1 lb penne
1 l | 35 fl. oz vegetable stock or water
800 g | 1 ¾ lbs | 4 cups
canned tomatoes
50 g | 2 oz sundried tomatoes
1 tsp basil
1 tsp oregano
1 handful baby spinach
1 tbsp parsley, chopped
200 g | 7 oz mozzarella cheese, sliced
50 g | 2 oz | ½ cup grated Parmesan

Method:

Heat the oven to 200°C (180° fan) 400F, gas 6.

Place the penne, tomatoes, spinach and herbs in an ovenproof dish and mix well. Pour over the stock or water.

Bake in the oven for 15 minutes, then scatter the Parmesan on top and layer the mozzarella, then cook for another 5-10 minutes, until the pasta is cooked.

Pork fillet with pineapple

Prep and cook time: 20 minutes
serves: 4

Ingredients:
45 ml | 1 ½ fl. oz sunflower oil
2 cloves of garlic, crushed
2 red chillies, chopped
600 g | 1 ¼ lbs pork fillet, chopped
1 red onion, sliced
1 red pepper, chopped
2 stalks celery
1 small tin pineapple chunks, drained
1 small tin bamboo shoots, drained
45 ml | 1 ½ fl. oz dark soy sauce
1 tbsp oyster sauce
spring onions (scallions)

Method:
Heat the oil in a wok on a high heat until it is smoking, then stir-fry the garlic and chilli for 2 minutes.

Add the pork, cook for 2 minutes then add the onion, pepper and celery and cook for 3 minutes, stirring all the time.

Add the pineapple, bamboo shoots, soy sauce and oyster sauce, cook for 2 minutes. Remove the celery stalks, and garnish with the spring onions. Serve immediately with rice or noodles.

Chicken and almond salad

Prep and cook time: 10 minutes
serves: 4

Ingredients:
1 large bunch flat leaf parsley
300 g | 10 oz mixed salad leaves
150 g | 5 oz | 2 cups flaked (slivered) almond, toasted
400 g | 14 oz cooked chicken, torn into strips
2 cloves of garlic, sliced
60 ml | 2 fl. oz olive oil
30 ml | 1 fl. oz lemon juice

Method:
Wash the parsley and mixed salad leaves thoroughly, pat dry and break into small sprigs.

Place the leaves into serving bowls and scatter over the chicken and almonds.

Mix the oil, lemon juice and garlic together, season with salt and pepper and drizzle over the salad leaves. Coat the ingredients in the dressing and serve.

Pumpkin and courgette gratin

Prep and cook time: 1 hour
serves: 4

Ingredients:
75 ml | 2 ½ fl. oz olive oil
1 onion, chopped
2 cloves of garlic, chopped
800 g | 1 ¾ lbs tomatoes, canned
450 g | 1 lb pumpkin,
peeled and cut into cubes
2 courgettes (zucchini), sliced
150 g | 5 oz | 1 ½ cups grated cheese

Method:

Heat 3 tablespoons of the oil in an ovenproof pan or dish and gently cook the onions for 5-10 minutes until soft. Add the garlic, cook for 1 minute then add the tomatoes and cook over a gentle heat for 15 minutes or until the sauce is thick. Season the pan with salt and pepper and the put the sauce aside.

Heat the oven to 180°C (160° fan) 375F, gas 5. Heat the remaining oil in the dish over a medium heat and gently cook the pumpkin for 5 minutes. Add the courgettes, stir gently then pour over the tomato sauce.

Cover the pan with foil and bake in the oven for 15 minutes then scatter over the cheese, return to the oven uncovered and bake for a further 10-15 minutes or until the cheese has melted and the vegetables are tender.

Spicy chilli squid

Prep and cook time: 15 minutes
serves: 4

Ingredients:
45 ml | 1 ½ fl. oz sunflower oil
4 shallots, finely sliced
2 cloves of garlic, chopped
2 red chillies, finely chopped
700 g | 1 ½ lbs squid,
cleaned and prepared
30 ml | 1 fl. oz soy sauce
1 tbsp fish sauce
1 lime, juiced
1 tsp sugar
lime leaves

Method:
Heat the oil in a wok until it is smoking hot, then add the shallots, garlic and chilli.

Stir fry for 2 minutes then add the squid pieces and continue cooking over a high heat for 3 minutes, or until the squid is just tender. Do not overcook the squid or it will become tough.

Add the soy sauce, fish sauce, lime juice and sugar, stir quickly and serve immediately.

Orange and sultana couscous salad

Prep and cook time: 20 minutes
serves: 4 (as a side dish)

Ingredients:
225 g | 8 oz | 2 cups couscous
2 oranges, peeled
1 spring onion (scallion), finely sliced
150 g | 5 oz | 1 cup cashew nuts,
roughly chopped
150 g | 5 oz | 1 cup sultanas
150 g | 5 oz | 1 cup currants
1 lemon, juice and zest
30 ml | 1 fl. oz olive oil

Method:
Place the couscous in a pan with 2 cups of boiling water. Cover the pan and let it soak for 10 minutes then fluff it up with a fork.

Cut away the orange segments, leaving the membranes behind and reserving the juice. Set the segments aside.

Mix the remaining ingredients into the couscous, adding the orange segments and juice, and season with salt and pepper.

Mustard salmon with green beans

Prep and cook time: 30 minutes
serves: 4

Ingredients:
45 ml | 1 ½ fl. oz olive oil
30 g | 1 oz coarse grain mustard
4 salmon fillets, skin on
200 g | 7 oz green (string)
beans, trimmed
1 courgette (zucchini), sliced

Method:

Heat the oven to 200°C (180° fan) 400F, gas 6.

Mix the oil and mustard together, season with salt and pepper and brush over the salmon fillets.

Lay the beans and courgette slices on the bottom of an ovenproof dish.

Lay the salmon fillets on top of the vegetables, skin side down, and cover with foil. Bake in the oven for 10 minutes then remove the foil, return the dish to the oven and bake for a further 10-15 minutes, or until the salmon is cooked through.

Seafood paella

Prep and cook time: 40 minutes
serves: 4

Ingredients:
60 ml | 2 fl. oz olive oil
100 g | 3 ½ oz pancetta, cubed
1 onion, finely sliced
2 cloves of garlic, chopped
1 red pepper, sliced
225 g | 8 oz paella rice
125 ml | 4 ½ fl. oz | ½ cup white wine
2 pinches of saffron, dissolved in
boiling water
750 ml | 1 ½ lbs | 3 cups chicken stock
200 g | 7 oz squid rings, cleaned
150 g | 5 oz | 1 cup frozen peas
110 g | 4 oz clams, cleaned
110 g | 4 oz mussels, cleaned
12 tiger prawns
1 lemon, juiced

Method:
Heat the oil in a large pan and gently cook the pancetta until the fat starts to run. Add the onion and cook gently over a medium heat until soft.

Add the garlic and the pepper, cook for 2 minutes then add the rice and cook, stirring all the time, for 2 more minutes.

Add the wine, let bubble then add the saffron and stock. Cook over a low heat, stirring from time to time, for 15 minutes or until the rice is nearly tender. Add the squid rings and peas. Season with salt and pepper, heat through, then add the clams, mussels and prawns.

Stir very gently until the clams and mussels have opened and the squid and prawns are just cooked. Remove any mussels that haven't opened, squeeze over the lemon juice and serve immediately.

Baked sea bream with Mediterranean vegetables

Prep and cook time: 45 minutes
serves: 4

Ingredients:
900 g | 2 lbs sea bream,
scaled and cleaned
1 lemon, juiced
60 ml | 2 fl. oz olive oil
4 sprigs rosemary
4 sprigs thyme
1 lemon, sliced
3 cloves of garlic, sliced
2 small courgettes (zucchini), sliced
200 g | 7 oz cherry tomatoes
70 g | 2 ½ oz | ¾ cup pitted green
olives, sliced

Method:
Heat the oven to 200°C (180° fan) 400F, gas 6.

Wash the fish, pat dry and make 3 or 4 diagonal cuts on each side. Season the fish inside and out with salt and drizzle with the lemon juice and 2 tablespoons of the oil.

Tuck rosemary and thyme leaves into the slits of the fish and place the remainder with the lemon slices in the cavity.

Lay the courgette slices in the bottom of a greased ovenproof dish, overlapping as you go, place the fish on top and scatter the tomatoes around. Place the garlic slices on top.

Drizzle over the remaining oil, cover with foil and bake in the oven for 15 minutes. Scatter over the olives, return the dish to the oven and bake for a further 10-15 minutes, or until the fish is cooked through.

Stir-fried beef with peppers

Prep and cook time: 15 minutes
serves: 4

Ingredients:
60 ml | 2 fl. oz sunflower oil
3 cloves of garlic, crushed
2 tsp chilli powder
400 g | 14 oz beef fillet, sliced
1 onion, roughly chopped
1 red pepper, chopped
1 green pepper, chopped
1 yellow pepper, chopped
60 ml | 2 fl. oz dark soy sauce
30 ml | 1 fl. oz dry sherry
30 ml | 1 fl. oz soy sauce
30 ml | 1 fl. oz sesame oil
a pinch of sugar

Method:
Heat the oil in a wok until smoking hot then add the garlic and chilli powder and stir-fry for 2 minutes.

Add the beef and cook for 3 minutes then remove the beef from the pan and set aside.

Add a little more oil to the wok then add the onion and chopped peppers. Cook over a high heat, stirring all the time, for 5 minutes then add the remaining ingredients and return the beef to the wok.

Stir-fry for 2 more minutes, season the dish with salt and pepper and serve immediately with sticky rice.

Pumpkin with chestnuts and onions

Prep and cook time: 40 minutes
serves: 4

Ingredients:
45 g | 1 ½ oz butter
1 tbsp sunflower oil
2 red onions, peeled and
cut into wedges
800 g | 1 ¾ lbs pumpkin or squash,
cut into bite-size pieces
250 g | 9 oz cooked chestnuts
3 tsp thyme leaves
80 ml | 2 ½ fl. oz vegetable stock

Method:
Heat the butter and oil in a wide pan, add the onions and cook gently over a low heat until soft but not brown.

Add the pumpkin, chestnuts, thyme and vegetable stock. Cover the dish and cook for 15-20 minutes, stirring occasionally, until the pumpkin is tender and golden brown.

Season the dish to taste with salt and pepper and serve immediately.

super soups.

Cream of pumpkin soup

Prep and cook time: 40 minutes
serves: 4

Ingredients:
30 ml | 1 fl. oz oil
30 g | 1 oz butter
1 tsp dried sage
1 onion, chopped
2 cloves of garlic, chopped
900 g | 2 lbs pumpkin,
peeled and chopped
750 ml | 27 fl. oz | 3 cups
vegetable stock
250 ml | 9 fl. oz | 1 cup cream
sage leaves, to garnish
50 ml | 2 fl. oz cream

Method:

Heat the oil and butter in a large pan and gently cook the onion for 10 minutes, on a medium heat until soft but not brown.

Add the garlic, cook for 1 minute then add the sage and pumpkin and stir well.

Pour over the stock, season with salt and pepper and increase the heat to boiling point. Turn the heat down and simmer gently for 20 minutes or until the pumpkin is tender, then blend with a hand blender until very smooth. For an extra silky texture, pass the soup through a fine sieve into a clean pan.

Stir in the cream, reheat gently and then serve garnished with sage leaves and a swirl of cream.

Chicken laksa

Prep and cook time: 40 minutes
serves: 4

Ingredients:
30 ml | 1 fl. oz vegetable oil
1 onion, finely chopped
1 clove of garlic, finely chopped
45 g | 1 ½ oz yellow curry paste
2 large chicken breasts, cut into chunks
500 ml | 18 fl. oz | 2 cups chicken stock
400 ml | 14 fl. oz | 1 ⅔ cups
coconut milk
1 tbsp fish sauce
1 lime, juiced
200 g | 7 oz rice noodles,
cooked according to instructions
2 red chillies, sliced
1 tomato, sliced
coriander (cilantro) leaves
bean sprouts
lime slices

Method:
Heat the oil in a large pan and gently cook the onion and garlic over a medium heat until soft but not brown.

Stir in the curry paste, cook for 2 minutes then add the chicken, stock and coconut milk.

Increase the heat to boiling point then reduce it to simmer gently for 25 minutes. Add the fish sauce and lime juice, season with salt and pepper and pour into warmed bowls.

Add the noodles to the bowls then scatter over the sliced chillies, tomato and coriander leaves. Serve with bean sprouts and lime slices.

Red lentil soup

Prep and cook time: 20 minutes
serves: 4

Ingredients:
60 ml | 2 fl. oz oil
1 onion, finely sliced
2 cloves of garlic, chopped
2 tbsp fresh ginger, peeled
and chopped
1 red chilli, chopped
2 tsp curry powder
1 tsp turmeric
300 g | 11 oz | 1 ½ cups red lentils
200 g | 7 oz | 1 cup canned
tomatoes, chopped
750 ml | 26 fl. oz | 3 cups chicken stock
2 spring onions (scallions),
sliced diagonally
2 tbsp coriander (cilantro), chopped

Method:
Heat the oil in a deep pan and fry the onions until soft
but not brown.

Add the garlic, ginger, chilli pepper, curry powder and
turmeric and cook for 2 minutes then add the lentils and
stir well.

Add the tomatoes and stock, season the pan with salt and
pepper and simmer very gently for 30 minutes, or until the
lentils are tender.

Serve garnished with the spring onions and coriander.

Hearty fish soup

Prep and cook time: 45 minutes
serves: 4-6

Ingredients:
30 ml | 1 fl. oz olive oil
2 onions, finely sliced
3 cloves of garlic, finely chopped
1 red chilli, finely chopped
a small pinch of saffron threads
400 g | 14 oz | 2 cups
tomatoes, canned
1 tbsp tomato puree
200 ml | 7 fl. oz | ⅞ cup dry white wine
450 g | 1 lb waxy potatoes,
peeled and diced
450 g | 1 lb mixed seafood- mussels,
clams, prawns (shrimp), squid
450 g | 1 lb haddock fillets,
cut into chunks
1 tbsp parsley, chopped

Method:
Heat the olive oil in a large pan and gently cook the onions over a medium heat until soft.

Add the garlic, chilli and saffron threads and cook for 2 minutes. Add the tomatoes, tomato paste and white wine. Increase the heat to boiling point, then reduce it down, add the potatoes and simmer gently for 20 minutes.

Wash and clean the seafood and fish fillets and add to the soup. Cover and simmer for a further 10 minutes then serve garnished with chopped parsley.

Chickpea soup

Prep and cook time: 30 minutes
serves: 4

Ingredients:
2 tbsp oil
1 tbsp butter
1 onion, finely chopped
2 cloves of garlic, finely chopped
1 tsp ground cumin
1 tsp turmeric
400 g | 14 oz | 2 cups canned
chickpeas (garbanzos), drained
750 ml | 26 fl. oz | 3 cups
vegetable stock
60 ml | 2 fl. oz sour cream

Method:
Heat the oil and butter in a large pan and gently cook the onions for 10 minutes on a low heat, until soft but not brown.

Add the garlic, cumin and turmeric, cook for 2 minutes then add the chickpeas and the stock. Increase the heat to boiling point and then simmer for 15 minutes.

Remove 4 tablespoons of the chickpeas to garnish, then puree the mixture with a hand blender, or in a food processor to a desired thickness. Add a little more stock, or water if the soup is too thick. Gently reheat, add 2 tablespoons of the sour cream and season with salt and pepper.

Pour into bowls and garnish with the remaining chickpeas and sour cream.

Mulligatawny

Prep and cook time: 40 minutes
serves: 4

Ingredients:
45 ml | 1 ½ fl. oz oil
2 onions, finely chopped
2 cloves of garlic, chopped
2 tbsp fresh ginger, peeled and grated
1 tsp chilli powder
1 tsp turmeric
1 tsp ground coriander
1 tsp garam masala
2 carrots, peeled and diced
4 tomatoes, skinned and chopped
750 ml | 26 fl. oz | 3 cups chicken stock
2 large chicken breasts, skinned and
cut into chunks
125 ml | 4 ½ fl. oz | ½ cup coconut milk
1 tbsp lemon juice
30 g | 1 oz flaked (slivered)
almonds, toasted
2 tbsp coriander (cilantro), chopped

Method:
Heat the oil in a large pan and gently cook the onions for
10 minutes on a low heat until soft.

Add the garlic, ginger, chilli powder, turmeric, ground
coriander and garam masala. Cook for 2 minutes, stirring all
the time, then add the carrots and tomatoes.

Pour over the stock and simmer for 10 minutes. Add the
chicken, simmer for 10 minutes then add the coconut milk
and simmer for 5 more minutes.

Stir in the lemon juice, season with salt and pepper and
then add the almonds and coriander leaves.

Indian chicken and vegetable soup

Prep and cook time: 40 minutes
serves: 4

Ingredients:
45 ml | 1 ½ fl. oz oil
1 onion, chopped
1 small leek, chopped
2 cloves of garlic, chopped
2 tsp curry powder
1 tsp paprika
2 large potatoes, peeled and chopped
2 carrots, peeled and chopped
1 courgette (zucchini), chopped
750 ml | 26 fl. oz | 3 cups
vegetable stock
250 ml | 9 fl. oz | 1 cup coconut milk
2 chicken breasts, skinned and
cut into strips
150 g | 5 oz | 1 cup frozen peas
mini poppadums, to serve

Method:
Heat the oil in a large pan and gently cook the onion and leek over a low heat, until soft but not brown.

Add the garlic, curry powder and paprika, cook for 1 minute then add the potatoes and carrots. Cook for 2 minutes, stirring all the time.

Add the courgette and vegetable stock, increase the heat to boiling point and then simmer for 15 minutes.

Add the coconut milk, increase the heat and then add the chicken and simmer for 5 minutes. Add the peas and simmer until the chicken is cooked through.

Season with salt and pepper and serve with the mini poppadums.

Vietnamese beef noodle soup

Prep and cook time: 20 minutes
serves: 4

Ingredients:
1 ½ l | 53 fl. oz | 6 cups beef stock
1 stick cinnamon
2 star anise
2 limes, juiced
30 ml | 1 fl. oz fish sauce
1 tbsp light soy sauce
1 tsp sugar
600 g | 1 ¼ lbs beef fillet, finely sliced
200 g | 7 oz rice noodles, soaked
according to packet instructions
100 g | 3 ½ oz | 1 cup bean sprouts
4 spring onions (scallions), finely sliced
2 red chillies, finely sliced
fresh coriander (cilantro)
2 limes

Method:
Place the stock in a large pan with the cinnamon and star anise and increase the heat.

Simmer for 5 minutes then add the lime juice, fish sauce, soy sauce and sugar and simmer for 5 more minutes.

Add the beef, noodles, spring onions and chilli, simmer for 5 minutes or until the beef is just cooked. Check the seasoning and serve with the coriander and lime slices.

Carrot soup

Prep and cook time: 30 minutes
serves: 4

Ingredients:
2 tbsp oil
30 g | 1 oz butter
1 onion, chopped
1 stalk celery, chopped
2 cloves of garlic, chopped
1 tsp ground cumin
1 tsp ground coriander
750 g | 1 ½ lbs carrots,
peeled and chopped
1 l | 35 fl. oz | 4 cups vegetable stock
1 tbsp parsley, chopped
1 tsp ground black pepper

Method:

Heat the oil and butter in a large pan and gently cook the onion and celery over a medium heat, until soft but not brown.

Add the garlic, cumin and coriander and cook for 2 minutes then add the carrots and stir well.

Pour over the stock, increase the heat to boiling point, then season the pan with salt and pepper and gently simmer for 15-20 minutes or until the carrots are very tender.

Puree with a hand blender until smooth then garnish with chopped parsley and pepper.

Three bean soup

Prep and cook time: 30 minutes
serves: 4

Ingredients:
45 ml | 1 ½ fl. oz oil
1 onion, finely chopped
2 cloves of garlic, chopped
1 tsp paprika
1 large potato, peeled and chopped
200 g | 7 oz | 2 cups canned butterbeans (lima beans)
200 g | 7 oz | 2 cups canned borlotti beans
200 g | 7 oz | 2 cups canned chickpeas (garbanzos)
200 g | 7 oz | 2 cups tomatoes, canned
750 ml | 26 fl. oz | 3 cups vegetable stock
2 tbsp parsley, chopped
1 tbsp thyme, chopped

Method:
Heat the oil in a large pan and gently cook the onion over a low heat until soft but not brown.

Add the garlic and paprika, cook for 1 minute then stir in the potato.

Add the drained butterbeans, borlotti beans, chickpeas, tomatoes and stock. Season the pan with salt and pepper then increase the heat to boiling point, then simmer gently for 20 minutes.

Stir in the parsley and thyme and serve.

Chickpea soup

Prep and cook time: 30 minutes
serves: 4

Ingredients:

30 ml | 1 fl. oz olive oil
1 onion, diced
1 clove of garlic, chopped
1 red chilli, chopped
1 bay leaf
1 l | 35 fl. oz | 4 cups vegetable stock
1 small cabbage, shredded
400 g | 14 oz | 2 cups tomatoes, canned
400 g | 14 oz | 2 cups chickpeas (garbanzos)
2 tbsp parsley, chopped
100 g | 3 ½ oz | 1 cup grated Parmesan

Method:

Heat the oil in a pan and gently cook the onion over a low heat until soft but not brown. Add the garlic and chilli and cook for 1 minute then add the bay leaf and pour over the stock or water.

Increase the heat to boiling point then add the cabbage, tomatoes and chickpeas, bring to a boil and simmer for 10 minutes or until the cabbage is tender.

Season the pan with salt and pepper and serve scattered with parsley and Parmesan.

Tomato soup

Prep and cook time: 40 minutes
serves: 4-6

Ingredients:
45 ml | 1 ½ fl. oz oil
2 onions, chopped
2 cloves of garlic, chopped
1 red chilli, deseeded and chopped
400 g | 14 oz | 2 cups tomatoes,
chopped
30 g | 1 oz tomato puree
600 ml | 21 fl. oz | 2 ½ cups
vegetable stock
2 tbsp fresh basil, chopped
1 tbsp fresh parsley, chopped
45 ml | 1 ½ fl. oz balsamic vinegar
1 tsp sugar
60 g | 2 oz crème fraiche
chives, chopped
extra virgin olive oil

Method:

Heat the oil in a large pan and gently fry the onion over a medium heat until soft. Add the garlic and chilli and cook for 2 more minutes.

Add the chopped tomatoes and tomato puree then pour on the stock. Stir in the basil, parsley and balsamic vinegar. Season the pan with salt, pepper and sugar.

Increase the heat to boiling point, then turn it down to simmer for 20-25 minutes, stirring occasionally.

Puree the soup with a hand blender until very smooth. Stir in the crème fraiche, reheat gently and check the seasoning.

Garnish the soup with chopped chives and drizzled with a little oil and serve with fresh crusty bread.

Sausage and white bean soup

Prep and cook time: 30 minutes
serves: 4

Ingredients:
45 ml | 1 ½ fl. oz oil
1 onion, finely chopped
1 stalk celery, finely chopped
2 cloves of garlic, finely chopped
2 carrots, finely chopped
1 l | 35 fl. oz | 4 cups vegetable stock
2 large pork sausages, sliced
400 g | 14 oz | 2 cups canned
haricot (navy) beans
fresh parsley, chopped

Method:
Heat the oil in a large pan and gently cook the onion and celery for 10 minutes until soft.

Add the garlic and carrots, cook for 2 minutes then add the stock. Bring to a boil and add the sausages then simmer for 15 minutes and add the drained beans.

Season with salt and freshly ground pepper, add the parsley and simmer for 5 more minutes.

Leek and potato soup

Prep and cook time: 40 minutes
serves: 4

Ingredients:
30 ml | 1 fl. oz oil
30 g | 1 oz butter
2 large leeks, finely chopped
2 large potatoes, peeled and chopped
750 ml | 26 fl. oz | 3 cups
vegetable stock
250 ml | 9 fl. oz | 1 cup cream
2 rashers bacon, chopped and fried
chives, to garnish

Method:
Heat the oil and butter and gently cook the leeks for 10 minutes over a low heat until soft but not brown.

Add the potatoes, stir for 2 minutes then add the stock. Increase the heat to boiling point then simmer for 25 minutes, or until the potatoes are very tender.

Blend in the pan with a hand blender then add the cream, season with salt and pepper and reheat gently.

Serve garnished with the bacon and chives.

Tomato, lentil and chilli soup

Prep and cook time: 40 minutes
serves: 4

Ingredients:
45 ml | 1 ½ fl. oz oil
1 onion, chopped
1 stick celery, chopped
1 clove of garlic, chopped
2 red chillies, chopped
2 tsp paprika
1 carrot, chopped
200 g | 7 oz | 1 cup red lentils, washed
250 ml | 9 fl. oz | 1 cup vegetable stock
800 g | 1 ¾ lbs | 4 cups
tomatoes, canned
1 tbsp chopped parsley
1 tbsp chopped thyme
45 ml | 1 ½ fl. oz yoghurt
12 king prawns

Method:

Heat the oil in a large pan and gently cook the onion and celery until soft but not brown.

Add the garlic and the chillies, cook for 1 minute then add the paprika and stir well.

Add the carrot and lentils, stir for 1 minute then add the stock and tomatoes. Season with salt and pepper, increase the heat to boiling point and then simmer gently for 20 minutes. Thread 4 skewers with the prawns and lightly grill them for 3-4 minutes each side or until cooked through.

Stir the parsley into the pot, the thyme and yoghurt. Check the seasoning and serve garnished with the remaining parsley and a grilled king prawn skewer.

Onion soup with mushrooms

Prep and cook time: 45 minutes
serves: 4

Ingredients:
30 ml | 1 fl. oz oil
60 g | 2 oz butter
4 large onions, thinly sliced
2 cloves of garlic, chopped
150 g | 5 oz button mushrooms, sliced
1 tbsp chopped thyme
250 ml | 9 fl. oz | 1 cup white wine
750 ml | 26 fl. oz | 3 cups chicken stock

Method:
Heat the oil and butter in a large pan and cook the onions very gently for 15 minutes, stirring from time to time.

Add the garlic and mushrooms, cook gently for 5 minutes then add the thyme and white wine.

Let the soup bubble then pour in the stock. Increase the heat to boiling point, season with salt and pepper and simmer gently for 20 minutes.

Pea soup with crayfish and mint

Prep and cook time: 1 hour and 20 minutes
serves: 4

Ingredients:
750 ml | 26 fl. oz | 3 cups
vegetable stock
1 large white onion, chopped
2 cloves of garlic, chopped
450 g | 1 lb | 3 cups peas,
fresh or frozen
1 tsp honey
1 tbsp lemon juice
200 g | 7 oz crayfish tails, cooked
2 tbsp sour cream
mint sprigs
cayenne pepper
pine nuts

Method:

Gently brown the onion in a tablespoon of oil, over a low heat until soft. Put the stock and garlic in the large pan and increase the heat to boiling point.

Add the peas and honey and simmer gently until the peas are tender, this will take about 15 minutes for fresh peas, 5 minutes for frozen peas.

Blend the soup with a hand blender in the pan, add the lemon juice and season with salt and pepper. Chill for at least 1 hour before serving.

To serve, ladle into bowls, add the crayfish, swirl in the sour cream and garnish with mint sprigs, cayenne pepper and pine nuts.

Autumnal mushroom soup

Prep and cook time: 30 minutes
serves: 4

Ingredients:
30 ml | 1 fl. oz oil
30 g | 1 oz butter
450 g | 1 lb mixed wild mushrooms
2 leeks, chopped
2 cloves of garlic, chopped
125 ml | 4 ½ fl. oz | ½ cup dry sherry
750 ml | 26 fl. oz | 3 cups chicken stock
250 ml | 9 fl. oz | 1 cup cream
2 tbsp chopped hazelnuts (cob nuts)

Method:

Heat the oil and butter in a large pan and gently fry the mushrooms until they are tender and lightly browned. Remove the mushrooms from the pan and set them aside.

Add the leek to the pan and cook gently over a low heat until they are soft but not brown, then add the garlic and cook for 1 minute.

Pour the sherry over the leeks, let it bubble then add the stock and increase the heat to boiling point. Turn the heat down and simmer gently for 15 minutes.

Return most of the mushrooms to the pan, reserving a few to garnish, and simmer for a further 5 minutes.

Blend the soup with a hand blender then stir in the cream. Season the pan with salt and pepper, heat through gently and serve garnished with the reserved mushrooms and chopped nuts.

Thai chicken and coconut soup

Prep and cook time: 30 minutes
serves: 4

Ingredients:
1 tbsp light sesame oil
1 onion, finely sliced
2 cloves of garlic, chopped
2 tbsp fresh ginger, grated
1 stalk lemongrass, finely chopped
2 red chillies, cut into strips
350 ml | 12 fl. oz | 1 ½ cups chicken stock
400 ml | 14 fl. oz | 1 ⅔ cups coconut milk
2 chicken breasts, skinned and cut into strips
6 lime leaves
30 ml | 1 fl. oz light soy sauce
1 tbsp fish sauce
1 tsp sugar
1 lime, juiced

Method:
Heat the oil in a large pan and gently fry the onion over a medium heat for 10 minutes until soft but not brown.

Add the garlic, ginger, lemongrass and chilli and cook for 1 minute.

Add the stock and coconut milk, increase the heat to boiling point then add the chicken and lime leaves and simmer for 15 minutes.

Add the soy sauce, fish sauce, sugar and lime juice. Stir the pan well and serve either on its own or with fresh rice noodles.

Pea soup

Prep and cook time: 30 minutes
serves: 4

Ingredients:
4 spring onions (scallions)
30 ml | 1 fl. oz oil
1 tbsp butter
1 clove of garlic, chopped
450 g | 1 lb | 3 cups frozen peas
600 ml | 21 fl. oz | 2 ½ cups
chicken stock
200 ml | 7 fl. oz | ⅞ cup cream
crème fraiche, to serve

Method:
Finely slice the spring onions, keeping the white and green parts separate.

Heat the oil and butter in a pan and gently cook the white parts of the spring onions until soft but not brown. Add the garlic, cook for 1 minute then add the peas and the stock.

Increase the heat to boiling point, season with salt and pepper and simmer for 10 minutes. Blend with a hand blender then add the cream and the green parts of the spring onions.

Reheat very gently and serve with a swirl of the crème fraiche.

Spicy sweet potato soup with ginger

Prep and cook time: 30 minutes
serves: 4

Ingredients:
30 ml | 1 fl. oz oil
2 onions, chopped
1 clove of garlic, chopped
2 tbsp fresh ginger, peeled and grated
1 red chilli, chopped
2 sweet potatoes, peeled and cubed
30 ml | 1 fl. oz sherry vinegar
1l | 35 fl. oz | 4 cups vegetable stock
100 ml | 3 ½ fl. oz sour cream
a pinch of cinnamon
75 g | 2 ½ oz | ¾ cup goat's cheese
1 lime, zested

Method:
Heat the oil in a saucepan and cook the onion over a medium heat until soft. Add the garlic, ginger and chilli and cook for 2 minutes.

Add the sweet potatoes, stir for 2 minutes then add the vinegar and the stock. Cover with a lid and simmer for about 15 minutes until the potatoes are soft.

Puree the soup with a hand blender, stir in the cream and gently reheat. Season the pan with salt, pepper and cinnamon.

Ladle the soup into bowls, crumble some goat's cheese over the top and garnish with the lime zest.

winter warmers.

Spicy pork ragout

Prep and cook time: 2 hours
serves: 4

Ingredients:

45 ml | 1 ½ fl. oz oil
900 g | 2 lbs pork shoulder,
cut into cubes
1 onion, chopped
1 stick celery, chopped
1 clove of garlic, chopped
1 tsp paprika
1 tsp cumin seeds
1 carrot, chopped
400 g | 14 oz | 2 cups canned
tomatoes, chopped
1 tbsp tomato puree
250 ml | 9 fl. oz | 1 cup red wine
250 ml | 9 fl. oz | 1 cup meat stock
1 tbsp parsley, chopped

Method:

Heat the oil in a large pan on a medium heat and brown the meat on all sides. Remove the meat from the pan and set aside.

Gently cook the onion and celery until soft for 5 minutes then add the garlic, paprika and cumin seeds.

Cook for 2 minutes then add the carrot, tomatoes and tomato puree. Return the meat to the pan, pour over the wine and let the pan simmer.

Add the stock and parsley, bring to a simmer and cook very gently for 1 ½ hours or until the meat is very tender. Add a little water during cooking if necessary.

Lamb shanks with puy lentils

Prep and cook time: 2 hours
serves: 4

Ingredients:
45 ml | 1 ½ fl. oz oil
4 lamb shanks
8 shallots, peeled
2 cloves of garlic, chopped
1 tsp cumin seeds, lightly crushed
1 tsp cinnamon
200 g | 7 oz | 1 cup puy lentils, washed
125 ml | 4 ½ fl. oz | ½ cup white wine
500 ml | 18 fl. oz | 2 cups lamb stock
2 preserved lemons, finely sliced
2 handfuls spinach, washed

Method:
Heat the oven to 180°C (160° fan) 375F, gas 6.

Heat the oil in a large ovenproof and flameproof pot and brown the lamb shanks on all sides. Remove the lamb from the pot and set aside.

Add the shallots to the pot, cook gently until they begin to soften then add the garlic, cumin and cinnamon.

Cook gently for 2 minutes then stir in the lentils. Return the lamb to the pot and pour over the wine and stock and season with salt and pepper.

Cover the pot with a lid and place in the oven for 1 ½ hours. Add the preserved lemons and the spinach then return the pot to the oven and continue cooking for 15 minutes, or until the lamb is very tender.

Ratatouille with chicken

Prep and cook time: 1 hour 15 minutes
serves: 4

Ingredients:
60 ml | 2 fl. oz olive oil
8 chicken legs
2 red onions, cut into wedges
4 cloves of garlic, chopped
1 tsp paprika
1 red pepper, chopped
1 aubergine (eggplant), sliced
2 courgettes (zucchini), chopped
1 tbsp tomato puree
250 ml | 9 fl. oz | 1 cup chicken stock
4 tomatoes, chopped
8 basil leaves

Method:

Heat the oven to 180°C (160° fan) 375F, gas 5. Heat the oil in a large ovenproof and flameproof pot and brown the chicken pieces on all sides. Remove the chicken from the pot and set aside.

Add the onions to the pot, cook gently for 5 minutes until soft then add the garlic and paprika. Cook for 2 minutes then add the pepper.

Add the aubergine, coat in the oil then add the courgettes. Stir in the tomato puree and pour over the stock, return the meat to the pan and season with salt and pepper.

Cover with a lid and place in the oven for 30 minutes then add the tomatoes and basil, return the pot to the oven and cook for a further 20 minutes.

Toad-in-the-hole

Prep and cook time: 55 minutes
serves: 4

Ingredients:
90 ml | 3 fl. oz oil
450 g | 1 lb pork sausages
225 g | 8 oz | 2 cups plain
(all-purpose) flour
a pinch of salt
2 eggs
600 ml | 21 fl. oz | 2 ½ cups milk

Method:
Heat the oven to 220°C (200° fan) 425F, gas 7.

Heat the oil in an ovenproof and flameproof dish on the hob and fry the sausages for 5 minutes until browned on all sides.

Put the flour and salt into a mixing bowl and make a well in the centre. Break in the eggs and gradually work in half the milk, beating until it is smooth. Beat in the rest of the milk.

Pour the batter into the dish with the sausages and bake in the oven for 20-30 minutes until risen and golden brown. Serve immediately with mashed potato and green beans.

Beef and bean stew

Prep and cook time: 1 hour and 30 minutes
serves: 4

Ingredients:
45 ml | 1 ½ fl. oz oil
900 g | 2 lbs braising beef,
cut into cubes
2 onions, chopped
2 cloves of garlic, chopped
2 tsp paprika
4 carrots, peeled and chopped
2 potatoes, peeled and chopped
30 g | 1 oz flour
45 g | 1 ½ oz tomato puree
500 ml | 18 fl. oz | 2 cups beef stock
green (string) beans, to serve

Method:

Heat the oil in a large pot and brown the meat over a medium heat.

Add the onions and garlic, coat them in the oil, then add the paprika, carrots and potatoes.

Sprinkle over the flour and stir well, then add the tomato puree and beef stock and season with salt and pepper. Increase the heat to boiling point, turn the heat down very low and simmer for 1 ¼ hours, stirring from time to time, or until the meat is very tender.

Serve with the green beans and mashed potato.

Risotto with asparagus, peas and beans

Prep and cook time: 35 minutes
serves: 4

Ingredients:
30 g | 1 oz butter
1 tbsp oil
2 shallots, finely chopped
200 g | 7 oz | 1 cup risotto rice
850 ml | 30 fl. oz | 3 ½ cups
vegetable stock
300 g | 11 oz | 2 cups frozen peas
2 tbsp mint, chopped
50 g | 2 oz | ½ cup grated Parmesan
12 runner (pole) beans
100 g | 3 ½ oz asparagus
1 bunch spring onions (scallions)

Method:
Heat the butter and oil in a wide pan and cook the shallots very gently for 10 minutes until soft but not brown.

Add the rice and stir until it becomes translucent, then add a ladle of stock and stir until it is absorbed by the rice.

Turn the heat down and continue adding the stock one ladle at a time, stirring constantly, until the rice has become creamy and just cooked. You may need to add a little more stock or water.

Add the peas, asparagus, beans, mint and Parmesan, season with salt and pepper and continue cooking for 5 minutes, or until the greens are cooked through. Sprinkle with the spring onions and serve.

Chicken and leek cobbler

Prep and cook time: 45 minutes
serves: 4

Ingredients:
45 ml | 1 ½ fl. oz oil
1 tbsp butter
2 leeks, sliced
2 cloves of garlic, sliced
1 carrots, chopped
2 large chicken breasts,
skinned and cut into chunks
125 ml | 4 ½ fl. oz | ½ cup white wine
125 ml | 4 ½ fl. oz | ½ cup
chicken stock
450 g | 1 lb puff pastry,
thawed if frozen
1 egg, beaten
50 g | 2 oz | ½ cup grated cheese

Method:
Heat the oven to 200°C (180°C fan) 400F, gas 6.

Heat the butter and oil in a large ovenproof and flameproof dish on the hob and gently cook the leeks until soft. Add the garlic and the carrot, cook for 2 minutes, then add the chicken.

Brown the meat lightly and add the wine, let it bubble then add the stock. Season with salt and pepper and simmer very gently for 10 minutes.

Roll out the pastry on a floured board to a thickness of 1 cm / ½" and cut out circles about 5 cm / 2" in size. Brush the circles with the beaten egg, scatter over the cheese and place on top of the dish.

Bake in the oven for 15-20 minutes and serve.

Baked macaroni cheese

Prep and cook time: 30 minutes
serves: 4

Ingredients:
25 g | 1 oz | ¼ stick butter
1 clove of garlic, finely sliced
2 tomatoes, sliced
750 g | 1 ½ lbs fresh macaroni
750 ml | 25 fl. oz | 3 cups readymade
cheese sauce
75 g | 2 ½ oz | 1 ½ cups fresh
coarse breadcrumbs
100 g | 3 ½ oz | 1 cup grated Parmesan

Method:
Heat the oven to 180°C (160° fan) 375F, gas 6.

Rub the butter over the base and sides of an ovenproof dish.

Scatter the garlic and tomato slices on the base of the dish and add the macaroni.

Pour over the sauce, scatter over the breadcrumbs and Parmesan and bake in the oven for 20-25 minutes.

Boeuf Bourguignon

Prep and cook time: 2 hours
serves: 4

Ingredients:
75 ml | 2 ½ fl. oz oil
800 g | 1 ¾ lbs braising beef,
cut into cubes
125 g | 4 ½ oz bacon, chopped
1 onion, chopped
1 stalk celery, chopped
2 cloves of garlic, chopped
2 carrots, cut into batons
200 g | 7 oz button mushrooms
500 ml | 18 fl. oz | 2 cups red wine
500 ml | 18 fl. oz | 2 cups beef stock
2 bay leaves
3-4 sprigs rosemary

Method:

Heat 2 tablespoons of the oil in a large pan over a medium heat and brown the meat on all sides. Remove from the pan and set aside.

Add the remaining oil to the pan and cook the bacon until the fat starts to run. Add the onion and celery and cook until softened.

Add the garlic, cook for 1 minute then add the carrots and mushrooms and cook until they begin to brown.

Return the meat to the pan then add the wine, stock, bay leaves and rosemary. Bring to a boil then turn the heat down and simmer very gently for 1 ½ - 2 hours, or until the meat is very tender.

Herb crusted leg of lamb

Prep and cook time: 3 hours
serves: 4-6

Ingredients:
45 ml | 1 ½ fl. oz oil
1 leg lamb
45 g | 1 ½ oz fresh rosemary, chopped
45 g | 1 ½ oz fresh thyme, chopped
8 cloves of garlic
3 bay leaves
2 sprigs thyme
3 sprigs fresh marjoram
45 ml | 1 ½ fl. oz balsamic vinegar

Method:

Heat the oven to 160°C (140° fan) 325F, gas 3. Rub the lamb with salt and pepper. Heat the oil in a roasting pan on the hob and brown the lamb joint on all sides.

Press the chopped rosemary and thyme onto the lamb and scatter around the garlic, bay leaves and thyme sprigs. Roast the lamb in the oven for about 2 ½ hours, basting from time to time.

Drizzle the balsamic vinegar over the meat and garnish with the marjoram before serving.

Chicken stew

Prep and cook time: 1 hour
serves: 4

Ingredients:
45 ml | 1 ½ fl. oz oil
2 onions, finely chopped
3 cloves of garlic, crushed
2 red chillies, sliced
½ tsp ground cardamom
1 tsp ground cinnamon
1 tsp ground cumin
1 tsp ground coriander
1 tbsp curry powder
1 tsp ground ginger
50 g | 2 oz | ⅓ cup ground almonds
400 ml | 14 fl. oz | 1 ⅔ cups
coconut milk
300 ml | 11 fl. oz | 1 ⅓ cups
chicken stock
2 large chicken breasts,
skinned and cut into chunks
2 tbsp shelled peanuts
fresh coriander (cilantro)
coconut shavings

Method:
Heat the oil in a large pan and gently cook the onion on a low heat until soft.

Add the garlic and chillies, cook for 1 minute then add the spices. Cook for 2 minutes, stirring all the time, then add the almonds, coconut milk and stock.

Increase the heat to boiling point then turn the heat down, add the chicken and simmer very gently for 20 minutes. Season the pan with salt and pepper and simmer for a further 10 minutes.

Serve in bowls, garnished with the peanuts, coriander and coconut shavings.

Boulangère potatoes

Prep and cook time: 1 hour 30 minutes
serves: 4

Ingredients:
50 g | 2 oz | ¼ cup butter, softened
1 clove of garlic, finely chopped
900 g | 2 lb potatoes, peeled and
very finely sliced
1 tbsp dried mixed herbs
500 ml | 18 fl. oz | 2 cups
vegetable stock
50 g | 2 oz | ½ cup cheese, grated

Method:
Preheat the oven to 180°C (160° fan) 375F, gas 5.

Grease the inside of a large ovenproof dish with a little of the butter and scatter in the garlic.

Layer the potatoes into the dish, dotting with butter and seasoning with the herbs, salt and pepper as you go.

Pour in the stock, cover with foil and bake in the oven for 1 hour.

Remove the foil, scatter over the cheese if using, and return to the oven for 20 minutes, or until the potatoes are golden brown.

Coq au vin

Prep and cook time: 1 hour 10 minutes
serves: 4

Ingredients:
30 ml | 1 fl. oz oil
30 g | 1 oz butter
4 large chicken legs
125 g | 4 ½ oz | ½ cup bacon, chopped
225 g | 8 oz shallots, peeled
2 cloves of garlic, chopped
225 g | 8 oz small chestnut mushrooms
500 ml | 18 fl. oz | 2 cups white wine
1 tbsp fresh thyme leaves, chopped

Method:
Heat the oil and butter in a wide pan and brown the chicken legs on all sides. Remove the chicken from the pan and set aside.

Cook the bacon in the pan for 5 minutes until the fat begins to run, then add the shallots and cook until they start to soften.

Add the garlic, cook for one minute then add the mushroom and coat in the pan juices.

Return the chicken to the pan, pour over the wine and let it bubble. Turn the heat down, season with salt and pepper and cover with a lid or foil. Simmer very gently for 45-50 minutes or until the chicken is cooked through, stir in the fresh thyme leaves and serve with mashed potato and green beans.

Pumpkin risotto

Prep and cook time: 40 minutes
serves: 4

Ingredients:
30 g | 1 oz butter
1 tbsp oil
4 sage leaves
450 g | 1 lb pumpkin, peeled and diced
2 shallots, finely chopped
200 g | 7 oz | 1 cup risotto rice
850 ml | 30 fl. oz | 3 ½ cups
vegetable stock
50 g | 2 oz | ½ cup grated Parmesan

Method:
Heat the butter and oil in a wide pan and cook the sage leaves until crisp. Remove from the pan and set aside.

Cook the diced pumpkin in the pan until lightly browned then remove about 4 tablespoons and set aside to use a garnish.

Add the shallots to the pan and cook very gently for 5 minutes until soft but not brown.

Add the rice and stir until the rice becomes translucent, then add a ladle of stock and stir until it is absorbed. Turn the heat down and continue adding the stock one ladle at a time, stirring constantly, until the rice has become creamy and just cooked.

Season with salt and pepper and mix in the reserved pumpkin. Sprinkle with the Parmesan and sage leaves.

Oven-baked garlic chicken

Prep and cook time: 45 minutes
serves: 4

Ingredients:
30 ml | 1 fl. oz oil
4 chicken legs, jointed
4 small potatoes, scrubbed and
cut into wedges
2 onions, cut into wedges
2 cloves of garlic, thinly sliced
2 lemons, cut into wedges
1 bunch thyme
175 ml | 6 fl. oz | ¾ cup
chicken stock or water

Method:

Heat the oven to 200°C (180° fan) 400F, gas 6.

Heat the oil in an ovenproof and flameproof dish on the hob and brown the chicken pieces on all sides. Remove the chicken from the pan and set aside.

Add the potatoes, onions, garlic and lemons to the dish and coat them in the oil then return the chicken and scatter over the thyme.

Season the dish with salt and pepper, pour over the stock and cover with foil. Place in the oven and roast for about 20 minutes and then remove the foil, baste the chicken and vegetables with the juices and continue cooking until the chicken is golden brown and cooked through, for another 10-15 minutes.

Japanese soba noodles with seafood

Prep and cook time: 30 minutes
serves: 4

Ingredients:
150 g | 5 oz squid, cleaned
1 ½ l | 53 fl. oz | 6 cups chicken stock
2 tbsp fresh ginger, peeled thinly sliced
25 g | 1 oz dried shitake mushrooms, soaked in water
45 ml | 1 ½ fl. oz light soy sauce
30 ml | 1 fl. oz dry sherry
1 red pepper, thinly sliced
8 scallops
4 king prawns, peeled
150 g | 5 oz mange tout (snow peas)
1 handful bean sprouts
200 g | 7 oz soba noodles, cooked according to packet instructions
1 lime, juiced

Method:

Score the squid in a cross-cross pattern and cut the flesh into strips, then set it aside.

Heat the stock in a large pan and add the ginger then increase the heat to boiling point.

Slice the mushrooms and add them to the pan with their soaking liquid. Add the soy sauce, sherry and the pepper.

Simmer for 10 minutes then add the scallops, followed by the king prawns, mange tout, bean sprouts, noodles and lime juice.

Simmer the dish for 5 minutes then add the squid. Continue cooking very gently for 2 minutes, add any salt or pepper as needed and serve immediately.

Braised lamb shanks

Prep and cook time: 2 hours 30 minutes
serves: 4

Ingredients:
30 ml | 1 fl. oz oil
4 lamb shanks
1 large onion, peeled and diced
1 carrot, peeled and diced
1 garlic clove, crushed
250 ml | 9 fl. oz | 1 cup red wine
2 tbsp tomato puree
400 ml | 14 fl. oz | 1 ⅔ cups meat stock
4 fresh bay leaves
3 sprigs thyme
boiled potatoes, to serve

Method:

Heat the oven to 150°C (130° fan) 300F, gas 2.

Heat the oil in a large ovenproof dish and brown the lamb shanks on all sides over a medium heat. Remove from the dish and set aside.

Gently cook the onion, garlic and carrot until softened then add the wine, let it bubble and stir in the tomato puree.

Return the lamb shanks to the dish, pour over the stock and add the bay leaves and thyme. Cover with a lid or tin foil, transfer to the oven and cook for 2 hours, or until the meat is very tender, basting the meat from time to time.

Remove the meat and vegetables from the pan with a slotted spoon and keep warm. Place the dish on the hob and reduce the sauce until thick and glossy. Season with salt and pepper and return the meat and vegetables to the pan.

Serve with boiled potatoes and garnished with the herbs.

Braised beef and vegetable stew

Prep and cook time: 1 hour 45 minutes
serves: 4

Ingredients:
45 ml | 1 ½ fl. oz oil
900 g | 2 lbs braising beef,
cut into chunks
8 shallots, peeled
2 cloves of garlic, chopped
1 tsp cayenne pepper
1 tsp ground cumin
750 ml | 26 fl. oz | 3 cups beef stock
200 g | 7 oz | 1 cup tomatoes, canned
300 g | 10 ½ oz new potatoes, scrubbed
400 g | 14 oz baby carrots, peeled
200 g | 7 oz green (string)
beans, trimmed
butter beans
400 g | 14 oz | 2 cups, canned
2 tbsp parsley, chopped

Method:
Heat the oil in a large pan and brown the meat on all sides over a medium heat. Remove the meat from the pan and set aside.

Gently cook the shallots in the pan until they start to take colour then add the garlic, cayenne pepper and cumin and cook for 2 minutes.

Return the meat to the pan and add the stock and tomatoes and turn up the heat. Season the pan with salt and pepper then simmer very gently for 45 minutes. Add the potatoes to the pan, cook for 10 minutes then add the carrots and cook for a further 10 minutes.

Add the green beans, butter beans and parsley and cook for 15 minutes.

Oven-roasted chicken with tomatoes

Prep and cook time: 1 hour 10 minutes
serves: 4

Ingredients:
45 ml | 1 ½ fl. oz oil
45 g | 1 ½ oz oil butter
4 large chicken legs
8 cloves of garlic, in their skins
500 g | 18 oz cherry (cocktail)
tomatoes, on the vine
3 sprigs thyme
125 ml | 4 ½ fl. oz | ½ cup white wine

Method:

Preheat the oven to 200°F (180° fan) 400F, gas 6.

Heat the oil and butter in an ovenproof and flameproof dish on the hob. Rub the chicken pieces with salt and pepper and brown on all sides.

Add the garlic, tomatoes and thyme and pour over the wine. Let the juices bubble, then baste everything with the juices, cover with foil and roast in the oven for 30 minutes.

Remove the foil then baste again and roast for a further 20 minutes, or until the chicken is cooked through.

Lamb ragout

Prep and cook time: 2 hours
serves: 4

Ingredients:
45 ml | 1 ½ fl. oz oil
900 g | 2 lb lamb shoulder,
cut into large cubes
2 onions, chopped
1 clove of garlic, chopped
1 tsp cumin seeds
1 tsp paprika
1 tsp turmeric
400 g | 14 oz | 2 cups
tomatoes, canned
250 ml | 9 fl. oz | 1 cup lamb stock
2 sprigs thyme
4 bay leaves
100 g | 3 ½ oz | 1 cup broad (fava)
beans, cooked and skinned

Method:
Heat the oil in a large pan on a medium heat and brown the meat on all sides.

Add the onions and cook gently for 5 minutes until soft then add the garlic, cumin seeds, paprika and turmeric.

Cook for 2 minutes then add the tomatoes, stock, thyme and bay leaves. Season with salt and pepper, increase the heat to boiling point and simmer very gently for 1 ½ hours, or until the meat is very tender. Add a little water if the pan becomes too dry.

Serve with the beans scattered over, with rice or tagliatelle.

Chorizo stew

Prep and cook time: 1 hour
serves: 4

Ingredients:
45 ml | 1 ½ fl. oz oil
2 onions, roughly sliced
4 cloves of garlic, sliced
2 tsp paprika
a small pinch of saffron
250 g | 9 oz chorizo, chopped
2 potatoes, peeled and diced
4 small carrots, peeled and chopped
45 g | 1 ½ oz tomato puree
675 ml | 24 fl. oz | 3 cups
vegetable stock
225 ml | 8 fl. oz | 1 cup red wine
1 bay leaf
1-2 tsp dried oregano
4 tbsp crème fraiche
parsley leaves, to garnish

Method:

Heat the oil in a large pan and gently cook the onions over a medium heat, until soft but not brown.

Add the garlic and paprika, cook for 2 minutes then add the chorizo and cook until the fat starts to run.

Add the potatoes and carrot, stir in the tomato paste then add then stock, wine, bay leaf and oregano.

Increase the heat to boiling point and season with salt and pepper, then turn the heat down and simmer gently for 35-40 minutes.

Spoon over the crème fraiche and garnish with the parsley.

hot 'n spicy.

Chicken curry with peanuts

Prep and cook time: 50 minutes
serves: 4

Ingredients:
45 ml | 1 ½ fl. oz oil
4 chicken legs, jointed
1 onion, finely chopped
1 clove of garlic, finely chopped
1 tbsp curry powder
1 tsp cayenne pepper
100 g | 3 ½ oz | 1 cup peanuts,
chopped
1 tbsp peanut butter
250 ml | 9 fl. oz | 1 cup chicken stock
4 large tomatoes, chopped
fresh coriander (cilantro)

Method:
Heat 1 tablespoon of the oil in a wide pan and brown
the chicken pieces on all sides, then take out of the pan
and set aside.

Add the rest of the oil to the pan and gently cook the
onion and garlic over a medium heat until soft.

Stir in the curry powder, cayenne pepper, peanuts and
peanut butter and add the stock. Return the chicken to the
pan, cover and cook for 30 minutes, turning occasionally.

Add the tomatoes and cook for a further 5-10 minutes.
Season the dish to taste with salt and pepper and serve
garnished with coriander.

Meatball tagine

Prep and cook time: 1 hour
serves: 4

Ingredients:
600 g | 1 ¼ lbs minced (ground) beef
90 g | 3 oz breadcrumbs
5 eggs
90 g | 3 oz fresh parsley, chopped
45 ml | 1 ½ fl. oz oil
1 onion, finely chopped
2 cloves of garlic, finely chopped
1 red chilli, finely chopped
1 tsp turmeric
2 tsp cumin
1 tsp paprika
400 g | 14 oz | 2 cups tomatoes, canned

Method:

Mix the beef with the breadcrumbs, one of the eggs, turmeric, cumin, paprika and half the parsley. Season the beef with salt and pepper and shape into meatballs.

Heat the oil in a wide pan and cook the meatballs until browned all over. Remove the meatballs from the pan and set aside.

Fry the onion, garlic and chilli pepper in the pan until soft, then add the tomatoes and remaining parsley and increase the heat to boiling point. Add the meatballs, cover and simmer very gently for 15-20 minutes, stirring from time to time.

Carefully crack the eggs into the pan, cover and cook for 5 minutes or until the eggs are set and serve immediately with cous cous or flatbreads.

Beef curry

Prep and cook time: 1 hour 30 minutes
serves: 4

Ingredients:
For the curry paste:
1 shallot, chopped
2 cloves of garlic, chopped
2 tbsp fresh galangal, peeled and
roughly chopped
2 red chillies, chopped
1 tsp shrimp paste

For the curry:
45 ml | 1 ½ fl. oz sesame oil
600 g | 1 ¼ lbs beef steak, sliced
2 shallots, finely sliced
2 cloves of garlic, finely chopped
800 ml | 28 fl. oz | 3 ½ cups coconut
milk
250 ml | 9 fl. oz | 1 cup beef stock
400 g | 14 oz potatoes, peeled and
chopped into large chunks
1 tbsp brown sugar
45 ml | 1 ½ fl. oz fish sauce
30 ml | 1 fl. oz lime juice
50 g | 2 oz | ½ cup peanuts, toasted
4 lime slices
1 tbsp coconut cream (optional)

Method:
Place all the curry paste ingredients in a food processor, or pestle and mortar and blend to a paste.

For the curry, heat the oil in a large pan or wok and quickly brown the beef on all sides. Remove the beef from the pan and set aside.

Add the shallots and garlic to the pan, cook for 2 minutes then stir in the curry paste. Cook for a further 2 minutes then return the meat to the pan and add the coconut milk, stock and potatoes.

Increase the heat to boiling point then turn down the heat and simmer gently for 20 minutes, or until the potatoes and beef are tender.

Add the sugar, fish sauce and lime juice, return to a simmer and season with salt and pepper.

Ladle the curry into warmed bowls, scatter over the peanuts and garnish with lime slices and coconut cream, if desired.

Duck curry with peaches and honey

Prep and cook time: 1 hour 30 minutes
serves: 4

Ingredients:
30 ml | 1 fl. oz soy sauce
30 ml | 1 fl. oz sesame oil
30 ml | 1 fl. oz honey
1 fresh chilli, deseeded and chopped
1 tsp chilli powder
1 tsp cinnamon
2 large duck breasts, skinned
and sliced
30 ml | 1 fl. oz sunflower oil
1 onion, chopped
2 cloves of garlic, chopped
1 tbsp sesame seeds
125 ml | 4 ½ fl. oz | ½ cup white wine
125 ml | 4 ½ fl. oz | ½ cup chicken
stock or water
125 ml | 4 ½ fl. oz | ½ cup coconut milk
75 g | 2 ½ oz | ½ cup almonds,
roughly chopped
2 ripe peaches, sliced
coriander (cilantro), chopped

Method:

Mix together the soy sauce, sesame oil, honey, chilli powder and cinnamon in a bowl. Add the sliced duck, mix well and set aside to marinade for 1 hour.

Heat the sunflower oil in a pan and gently fry the onion and garlic until soft but not brown.

Turn the heat to high, add the sliced duck and cook until the meat is brown all over.

Stir in the sesame seeds and add the wine, stock and coconut milk. Increase the heat to boiling point, then turn the heat down and simmer gently for 10 minutes.

Add the almonds and peaches, season with salt and pepper and simmer for 5 minutes, then add the sliced chilli and coriander. Serve immediately with Thai jasmine rice or noodles.

Jerk chicken

Prep and cook time: 3 hours
serves: 4

Ingredients:
1 onion, roughly chopped
2 tbsp fresh ginger, peeled
and chopped
2-3 green chillies, halved
2 tsp dried thyme
1 tsp grated nutmeg
a pinch of ground cinnamon
1 tsp allspice
½ tsp ground cloves
30 ml | 1 fl. oz sunflower oil
45 ml | 1 ½ fl. oz fresh lime juice
4 chicken legs
1 small pineapple, cut into
large wedges
2 limes, halved

Method:
Put all the marinade ingredients into a food processor and blend to make a fine paste. Rub the chicken with the marinade and set aside for at least 2 hours.

Preheat the oven to 200°C (180° fan) 400F, gas 6. Take the chicken out of the marinade, place it skin side up in a roasting pan and cook in the preheated oven for 20 minutes, turning once.

Add the pineapple and lime halves to the dish, turn the chicken skin side up again and continue to cook for another 20 minutes. Sprinkle the dish with chopped thyme leaves.

Serve the chicken on a bed of mixed wild rice with the pineapple.

Pumpkin curry with rice noodles

Prep and cook time: 30 minutes
serves: 4

Ingredients:
60 ml | 2 fl. oz oil
2 tbsp fresh ginger, peeled and grated
2 cloves of garlic, chopped
2 red chilli, finely chopped
1 tsp paprika
600 g | 1 ¼ lbs pumpkin,
peeled and chopped
500 ml | 18 fl. oz | 2 cups
vegetable stock or water
1 lime, juiced
200 g | 7 oz rice noodles,
soaked according to packet instructions
100 g | 3 ½ oz | 1 cup beansprouts
½ courgette, finely sliced
4 tomatoes, chopped
4 lime leaves, finely shredded
coriander (cilantro) leaves

Method:
Heat the oil in a large pan and gently cook the ginger, garlic, chilli and paprika for 2 minutes.

Add the pumpkin and stir well to coat with the spices then add the stock and increase the heat to boiling point. Allow the pumpkin to simmer for 20 minutes, or until it is tender and the liquid has been absorbed, stirring occasionally to prevent the pumpkin burning.

Season with salt and pepper and add the lime juice.

Serve the curry on a bed of rice noodles with the lime leaves and coriander leaves scattered over.

Thai yellow chicken curry

Prep and cook time: 1 hour
serves: 4

Ingredients:
30 ml | 1 fl. oz vegetable oil
2 tbsp fresh ginger, peeled and grated
2 cloves of garlic, crushed
1 stalk lemongrass, finely chopped
30 g | 1 oz yellow curry paste
500 ml | 18 fl. oz | 2 cups
chicken stock
500 ml | 18 fl. oz | 2 cups
coconut milk
1 lime, juiced
2 large chicken breasts, skinned
45 ml | 1 ½ fl. oz sesame oil
3 cloves of garlic, thinly sliced
2 red chillies, roughly chopped
60 ml | 2 fl. oz sweet chilli sauce
1 tbsp fish sauce
small bunch Thai basil leaves

Method:
Heat the vegetable oil in a large pan and gently fry the ginger, crushed garlic and lemongrass on a low heat.

Add the curry paste, stir for 2 minutes then pour in the stock and coconut milk.

Increase the heat to boiling point and then turn the heat down and simmer gently for 15 minutes. Add the lime juice and season with salt and pepper. Set aside and keep warm.

Flatten the chicken breasts with a meat hammer or rolling pin and cut it into strips.

Heat the sesame oil in the same pan and quickly fry the sliced garlic until it starts to brown. Add the chillies and chicken, cook for 2 minutes then add the chilli sauce and fish sauce.

Continue cooking, stirring all the time, until the chicken is cooked through. Stir in the Thai basil leaves and serve the chicken on top of the broth.

Lamb tagine

Prep and cook time: 1 hour 45 minutes
serves: 4

Ingredients:
45 ml | 1 ½ fl. oz oil
1 onion, finely chopped
2 cloves of garlic, chopped
2 tbsp fresh ginger, peeled and grated
1 tsp cayenne pepper
1 tsp paprika
1 tsp turmeric
2 tsp cinnamon
1 tsp black pepper
900 g | 2 lbs lamb shoulder,
cut into large cubes
1 tbsp honey
500 ml | 18 fl. oz | 2 cups lamb stock
175 g | 6 oz | 1 cup prunes, pitted
1 tbsp sesame seeds
fresh parsley, chopped

Method:
Heat the oil in a large pan and gently cook the onion and garlic on a medium heat until soft but not brown.

Add the ginger and the rest of the spices and cook for 2 minutes, stirring all the time.

Add the lamb, stir to coat the meat in the spice mixture then add the honey and lamb stock. Season with salt and pepper and increase the heat to boiling point, then cover and simmer very gently for 1 hour.

Add the prunes and simmer for a further 30 minutes or until the lamb is very tender. Serve with sesame seeds and the chopped parsley.

Potato curry with red lentils

Prep and cook time: 45 minutes
serves: 4

Ingredients:
60 ml | 2 fl. oz oil
1 onion, finely chopped
2 cloves of garlic, chopped
2 tbsp fresh ginger, grated
1 red chilli, deseeded and chopped
1 tsp ground coriander
1 tsp ground cumin
1 tsp curry powder
200 g | 7 oz | 1 cup red lentils,
washed and drained
450 g | 1 lb potatoes, peeled
and cut into chunks
2 tomatoes, skinned, deseeded
and chopped
poppadums, to serve

Method:
Heat the oil in a large pan and gently cook the onions
on a medium heat for 5 minutes until soft but not browned.
Add the garlic, ginger, chilli, ground coriander, cumin and
curry powder. Cook for 2 minutes then stir in the lentils.

Cook for 2 minutes then add 500 ml water, increase the heat
to boiling point and then add the potatoes and tomatoes.
Season with salt and pepper and simmer for 25 minutes or
until the potatoes and lentils are very tender.

Malaysian vegetable curry

Prep and cook time: 30 minutes
serves: 4

Ingredients:
45 ml | 1 ½ fl. oz oil
1 onion, chopped
2 cloves of garlic, chopped
1 tsp turmeric
30 g | 1 oz yellow curry paste
2 green and yellow peppers, sliced
250 ml | 9 fl. oz | 1 cup vegetable stock
250 ml | 9 fl. oz | 1 cup coconut milk
450 g | 1 lb new potatoes,
peeled and sliced
½ small white cabbage, shredded
1 lime, juiced

Method:
Heat the oil in a wide pan and gently cook the onion over a medium heat until soft.

Add the garlic, turmeric and curry paste and cook for 2 minutes, stirring all the time. Add the peppers, cook for 2 minutes then add the stock and coconut milk.

Increase the heat, add the potatoes and cook for 10 minutes. Add the cabbage and lime juice, season with salt and pepper and simmer for 5 more minutes, or until the potatoes are tender.

Spicy Moroccan kebabs

Prep and cook time: 2 hours 30 minutes
serves: 4

Ingredients:
2 shallots, peeled
3 cloves of garlic, peeled
2 red chillies, deseeded and chopped
1 tsp cumin seeds
1 tsp fennel seeds
1 small bunch coriander (cilantro)
45 ml | 1 ½ fl. oz oil
1 tsp lemon juice
60 ml | 2 fl. oz yoghurt
900 g | 2 lbs lamb shoulder,
cut into cubes

Method:

Place the shallots, garlic, chilli, cumin, fennel, coriander, oil, lemon juice and yoghurt into a food processor and blend until you have a paste.

Place the lamb cubes into a large bowl, mix in the paste and set aside to marinate for 2 hours.

Heat the barbecue or grill. Thread the lamb cubes onto metal skewers and cook for about 6 minutes, turning frequently.

Serve with flatbreads or couscous and salad.

Creole chicken with curried rice

Prep and cook time: 1 hour
serves: 4

Ingredients:
1 chicken, divided into 8 pieces
45 ml | 1 ½ fl. oz vegetable oil
1 tsp ground cumin
1 tbsp curry powder
3 cloves of garlic, finely chopped
250 ml | 9 fl. oz | 1 cup chicken stock
800 g | 1 ¾ lbs | 4 cups canned tomatoes, chopped
250 g | 9 oz mangetout (snow peas)
2 bay leaves
2 tbsp thyme leaves
1 tsp cayenne pepper
1 tbsp hot sauce
1 lemon, juiced

To serve:
200 g | 7 oz | 2 cups cooked white rice
200 g | 7 oz | 2 cups cooked saffron rice
pink peppercorns, lightly crushed

Method:
Rub salt and pepper into the chicken pieces. Heat the oil in a wide pan, cook the chicken pieces on a medium heat until they are browned all over, then sprinkle with cumin and curry powder, bay leaves, thyme leaves, cayenne pepper and cook for 3 minutes.

Add the garlic, lemon juice, hot sauce and stock, stir in the tomatoes and then season with salt and pepper, cover and simmer gently for 30 minutes, stirring from time to time.

Add the mangetout to the chicken and cook for a further 5 minutes. Mix the white and saffron rice together with the crushed pink peppercorns and serve.

Bobotie

Prep and cook time: 1 hour 15 minutes
serves: 4

Ingredients:
30 ml | 1 fl. oz oil
1 onion, chopped
2 cloves of garlic, chopped
45 g | 1 ½ oz madras curry paste
750 g | 1 ½ lb minced (ground) beef
2 slices white bread, soaked in milk
150 g | 5 oz | 1 cup whole almonds
150 g | 5 oz | 1 cup sultanas
2 bay leaves
250 ml | 9 fl. oz | 1 cup milk
3 eggs
1 tsp turmeric

Method:

Heat the oven to 175°C (150° fan) 350F, gas 4. Heat the oil in an ovenproof and flameproof dish and gently cook the onion and garlic on a medium heat until soft.

Stir in the curry paste, cook for 2 minutes then add the mince and cook for 3 more minutes.

Break up the soaked bread and add it to the dish with the almonds and sultanas. Mix it all together well and season with salt and pepper and add the bay leaves.

Mix together the milk, eggs and turmeric, pour the mixture over the meat and bake in the oven for 40 minutes or until the top is golden brown and the eggs have set.

Aubergine with harissa

Prep and cook time: 30 minutes
serves: 4, as a side

Ingredients:
2 large aubergines (eggplants), sliced
olive oil, for frying
30 g | 1 oz harissa paste
2 garlic cloves of, sliced
2 tomatoes, skinned and
finely chopped

Method:
Heat 1 cm / ½" oil in a frying pan to a high heat, taking care with hot oil. Fry the aubergine slices in batches for 3-4 minutes over a medium to high heat until golden brown, topping up the oil between batches as necessary. Drain on kitchen paper and set aside. Remove the oil from the pan and clean it.

Add a tablespoon of oil to the pan and fry the harissa paste, chopped tomato and garlic for 2 minutes. Add the aubergine slices, stir gently and set aside to cool before serving.

Lamb and apricot curry

Prep and cook time: 1 hour 15 minutes
serves: 4

Ingredients:
45 ml | 1 ½ fl. oz oil
1 onion, finely chopped
2 cloves of garlic, chopped
2 tsp cumin seeds
1 tsp curry powder
1 tsp paprika
800 g | 1 ½ lbs lamb, cubed
2 tomatoes, skinned and
finely chopped
375 ml | 13 fl. oz | 1 ½ cups
lamb stock or water
2 cinnamon sticks
150 g | 5 oz | 1 cup dried apricots,
roughly chopped
coriander (cilantro) leaves, to garnish

Method:
Heat the oil in a large pan and gently cook the onion until soft but not brown.

Add the garlic, cumin, curry powder and paprika, cook for 2 minutes then add the lamb, tomatoes and stock. Increase the heat to boiling point, add the cinnamon sticks then turn the heat down, cover and simmer for 1 hour.

Add the apricots, season with salt and pepper and continue cooking for 30 minutes or until the lamb is very tender. Add the coriander and serve with basmati rice.

Beef and pepper fajitas

Prep and cook time: 1 hour 25 minutes
serves: 4

Ingredients:
600 g | 1 ¼ lbs rump steak
45 ml | 1 ½ fl. oz sunflower oil
45 g | 1 ½ oz fajita seasoning mix
1 onion, sliced
1 red pepper, sliced
1 green pepper, sliced
1 lime, juiced
soft flour tortilla wraps, warmed
120 ml | 4 ½ fl. oz sour cream
cayenne pepper, to garnish
chilli sauce, to serve

Method:
Flatten the steak with a meat hammer or rolling pin and cut it into strips.

Mix the beef strips with the oil and fajita seasoning and set them aside to marinate for 1 hour.

Heat a wide pan until it is very hot and add the beef, onion and sliced peppers and cook, stirring all the time, for 5 minutes then stir in the lime juice.

Place the beef mixture on the tortilla wraps, drizzle over the sour cream and roll up. Garnish with a little cayenne pepper and serve with the chilli sauce.

Pork curry

Prep and cook time: 50 minutes
serves: 4

Ingredients:
450 g | 1 lb pork fillet
45 ml | 1 ½ fl. oz oil
1 onion, finely sliced
2 cloves of garlic, chopped
2 tbsp fresh ginger, cut into fine strips
1 green chilli, finely chopped
30 g | 1 oz yellow curry paste
500 ml | 18 fl. oz | 2 cups coconut milk
250 ml | 9 fl. oz | 1 cup chicken
stock or water
100 g | 3 ½ oz baby sweet corn
1 handful Thai basil leaves

Method:

Flatten the pork fillet with a meat hammer or rolling pin and cut it into thin slices.

Heat the oil in a wide pan and quickly fry the pork for a few minutes until it is evenly browned. Remove the meat from the pan and set aside.

Cook the chopped onion for 5 minutes over a medium heat until soft, then add the garlic, ginger and curry paste. Cook for 2 more minutes then stir in the coconut milk and stock. Increase the heat for a few minutes, and then simmer for 15 minutes until the meat is cooked through.

Season the pan with salt and pepper, stir in the basil leaves, baby sweet corn and cook for 2 more minutes.

Chicken and lemon tagine

Prep and cook time: 1 hour
serves: 4

Ingredients:
60 ml | 2 fl. oz olive oil
4 chicken legs, jointed
1 onion, chopped
2 cloves of garlic, chopped
2 tbsp fresh ginger, peeled and grated
a pinch of saffron, dissolved
in boiling water
60 ml | 2 fl. oz honey
2 preserved lemons, chopped
100 g | 3 ½ oz | 1 cup green
olives, chopped
2 tbsp coriander (cilantro), chopped

Method:
Heat the oil in a large pan and brown the chicken pieces on all sides. Remove the chicken from the pan and set aside.

Fry the onion in the pan on a low heat until soft but not brown, then add the garlic and ginger and cook for 2 minutes.

Return the chicken to the pan and add the saffron, honey and about 250 ml water. Increase the heat to boiling point and then turn the heat down, add the lemons and simmer for about 30 minutes, or until the chicken is cooked through.

Stir in the olives and coriander, season with salt and pepper and serve.

King prawn curry

Prep and cook time: 30 minutes
serves: 4

Ingredients:
45 ml | 1 ½ fl. oz sunflower oil
1 tsp turmeric
2 cloves of garlic
45 g | 1 ½ oz red curry paste
2 tbsp fresh ginger, peeled and grated
1 stalk lemongrass
125 ml | 4 ½ fl. oz | ½ cup fish stock
250 ml | 9 fl .oz | 1 cup coconut milk
1 lime, juiced
900 g | 2 lb king prawns, shelled
2 spring onions, thinly sliced diagonally

Method:

Heat the oil in a wide pan and stir in the garlic, lemongrass, ginger, turmeric and curry paste. Cook for 2 minutes then pour in the fish stock and coconut milk.

Increase the heat to boiling point, then turn the heat down and simmer for 10-15 minutes until the sauce has thickened.

Stir in the lime juice, season with salt and pepper and add the king prawns. Serve with Thai jasmine rice, garnished with the sliced spring onion.

Chicken laksa

**Prep and cook time: 30 minutes
serves: 4**

Ingredients:
3 red chillies, roughly chopped
4 cloves of garlic, chopped
2 tbsp fresh ginger,
peeled and chopped
4 shallots, peeled
1 tsp ground turmeric
2 coriander (cilantro), roughly chopped
45 ml | 1 ½ fl. oz oil
400 ml | 14 fl. oz | 1 ⅔ cups
coconut milk
400 ml | 14 fl. oz | 1 ⅔ cups
chicken stock
1 stalk lemongrass
3 chicken breasts, cut into strips
30 ml | 1 fl. oz fish sauce
1 tbsp light soy sauce
1 tsp sugar
1 handful baby spinach, chopped
150 g | 5 oz rice noodles, soaked
according to instructions
2 limes, juiced
lime leaves, to garnish
fresh coriander (cilantro)

Method:
Place the chillies, garlic, ginger, shallots, turmeric, coriander and oil in a food processor and pulse to make a fine paste.

Heat a large pan and gently fry the paste for 2 minutes, stirring all the time to prevent it burning.

Add the coconut milk, chicken stock and lemongrass. Increase the heat to boiling point, then add the chicken, fish sauce, soy sauce and sugar and simmer gently for 5 minutes, or until the chicken is cooked through.

Add the spinach, noodles and lime juice and cook for another minute, then serve garnished with lime leaves and coriander.

sweet treats.

Rhubarb crumble

Prep and cook time: 40 minutes
serves: 4

Ingredients:
500 g | 18 oz rhubarb, chopped
60 g | 2 oz caster (superfine) sugar
200 g | 7 oz | 2 cups flour
150 g | 5 oz | 1 ½ sticks butter
150 g | 5 oz | ¾ cup brown sugar

Method:
Heat the oven to 180°C (160° fan) 375F, gas 5. Place the rhubarb in an ovenproof dish and scatter over the caster sugar.

Place the flour, butter and brown sugar in a food processor and pulse until the mixture resembles fine breadcrumbs. If you do not have a food processor, rub the ingredients together with your fingertips until you reach the same breadcrumb consistency.

Scatter the mixture over the rhubarb and bake in the oven for 25-30 minutes, or until the top is golden brown and the filling is bubbling.

Winter trifle

Prep and cook time: 20 minutes
serves: 4

Ingredients:
6 trifle sponge cakes
30 ml | 1 fl. oz sweet sherry
600 g | 21 oz plums, stoned and stewed
500 ml | 18 fl. oz | 2 cups
ready-made custard
250 ml | 9 fl. oz | 1 cup single cream,
lightly whipped
35 g | 1 ¼ oz | ½ cup flaked
(slivered) almonds

Method:

Break up the trifle sponges and spread them over the base of a dish about 20 cm x 20 cm / 8" x 8" in size.

Drizzle over the sherry, then spoon over the plums in an even layer. Pour over the custard and top with the cream.

Chill until you are ready to serve the dessert, then scatter the almonds over the cream.

Baked fruit with cream

Prep and cook time: 30 minutes
serves: 4

Ingredients:
6 apricots, stones removed and halved
3 ripe white peaches, stones removed and quartered
200 g | 7 oz | 2 cups blackberries
200 ml | 7 fl. oz | ⅞ cup sweet white wine
4 vanilla pods (beans)
whipped cream
2 tsp cinnamon

Method:
Heat the oven to 200°C (180° fan) 400F, gas 6. Tear off 4 large sheets of foil and place in a roasting pan. Place 3 apricot halves and 3 peach quarters on each sheet and divide the blackberries between them, then sprinkle with 1 teaspoon of cinnamon.

Bring the edges of the foil together, pour a little wine into each parcel and tuck in a vanilla pod.

Pinch the edges of the foil together to make a tight seal and bake the parcels in the oven for 20-25 minutes.

Place the parcels on serving dishes and unwrap them. Serve with cream and a sprinkling of cinnamon.

Spiced pudding with treacle

Prep and cook time: 1 hour 30 minutes
serves: 4

Ingredients:
100 g | 3 ½ oz | 1 cup plain
(all-purpose) flour
1 tsp cinnamon
1 tsp mixed spice
1 ½ tsp baking powder
2 eggs
100 g | 3 ½ oz | ½ cup brown sugar
100 g | 3 ½ oz | 1 stick butter, softened
120 ml | 4 ½ fl. oz golden syrup,
plus more to serve

Method:
Heat the oven to 160°C (140° fan) 325F, gas 3.

Beat the flour, cinnamon, mixed spice, baking powder, eggs, sugar and butter together in a large bowl.

Butter a pudding mould and place spoon the golden syrup in the bottom. Pour the mixture into the mould then cover with a double layer of foil.

Place a rack in a deep roasting pan and fill the pan with boiling water to a depth of about 5 cm / 2". Place the mould on the rack and place in the oven. Bake for 1 hour, topping up the water if necessary. Test with a wooden toothpick, if it comes out clean, the pudding is done.

Allow it to cool a little, then turn the puddings out and pour over a little more syrup. Serve with ice-cream or custard.

Rhubarb pavlova

Prep and cook time: 1 hour
serves: 4

Ingredients:
3 egg whites
150 g | 5 oz | ⅔ cup caster
(superfine) sugar
250 ml | 9 fl. oz | 1 cup cream, whipped
450 g | 1 lb rhubarb, stewed

Method:
Heat the oven to 110°C (90° fan) 230F, gas 4.

Beat the egg whites until they form soft peaks, then beat in half the sugar a tablespoon at a time. Continue beating until the mixture becomes glossy and then fold in the remaining sugar.

Spread the mixture onto a baking sheet lined with baking parchment in a circle, making a wide well in the middle.

Bake in the oven for 40-50 minutes or until the meringue is firm but not brown.

Allow the meringue to cool then fill the middle with the whipped cream and top with the rhubarb.

Summer fruit pudding

Prep and cook time: 25 minutes
serves: 4

Ingredients:
250 g | 9 oz | 2 cups raspberries
200 g | 7 oz | 2 cups blackberries
2 peaches, stones removed
and flesh chopped
30 g | 1 oz sugar
425 ml | 15 fl. oz | 1 ¾ cups
canned custard
200 g | 7 oz plain vanilla sponge
100 g | 3 ½ oz white chocolate

Method:

Heat the oven to 180°C (160° fan) 375F, gas 5.

Spread the fruit into an ovenproof dish and scatter over the sugar. Cut the vanilla sponge into small chunks, break the white chocolate and scatter it over the fruit.

Pour over the custard and bake in the oven for 15-20 minutes.

Poached pears with chocolate sauce

Prep and cook time: 30 minutes
serves: 4

Ingredients:
500 ml | 18 fl. oz | 2 cups white wine
125 g | 4 ½ oz | ½ cup sugar
1 lemon, juiced
1 cinnamon stick
4 firm dessert pears
chocolate sauce

Method:

Place the wine, sugar, lemon juice and cinnamon stick in a large pan and increase the heat to boiling point.

Peel the pears, leaving the stalks intact and slice off the bottom to leave a firm base. Place the pears side by side in the pan, cover and simmer gently for 20-25 minutes or until the pears are soft.

Serve the pears drizzled with the chocolate sauce and ice-cream.

Apple and blackberry crumble

Prep and cook time: 40 minutes
serves: 4

Ingredients:
500 g | 18 oz dessert apples,
peeled and chopped
300 g | 11 oz blackberries
50 ml | 2 fl. oz apple juice
60 g | 2 oz sugar

For the crumble:
100 g | 3 ½ oz | 1 stick butter
100 g | 3 ½ oz | ½ cup brown sugar
50 g | 2 oz | ½ cup flour
75 g | 2 ½ oz | ½ cup ground almonds
120 g | 4 oz | ⅔ cup chopped
hazelnuts (cob nuts)
75 g | 2 ½ oz rolled oats

Method:
Preheat the oven to 200°C (180° fan) 400F, gas 6.

Put the apples and blackberries into an ovenproof dish with
the apple juice and sugar.

For the crumble, place the butter, sugar, flour and almonds
in a food processor and pulse until the mixture resembles
breadcrumbs then mix in the hazelnuts and oats. Alternatively,
rub the ingredients together with your fingertips until it reaches
the same consistency.

Sprinkle the crumble over the fruit and bake in the oven
for 20-25 minutes. Serve straight from the oven with ice-cream
or custard.

Rice pudding with plums

Prep and cook time: 1 hour
serves: 4

Ingredients:
25 g | 1 oz | ¼ stick butter
200 g | 7 oz | 1 cup pudding rice
750 ml | 26 fl. oz | 3 cups milk
60 g | 2 oz caster sugar
600 g | 1 ¼ lbs plums, stoned and
cut into wedges
30 g | 1 oz brown sugar
100 ml | 3 ½ fl. oz sweet white wine

Method:
Preheat the oven to 200°C (180° fan) 400F, gas 6.

Butter the base and sides of an ovenproof dish and add the rice, milk and sugar. Stir gently then cover with foil and bake in the oven for 20 minutes, stirring from time to time.

Arrange the plum wedges on top of the pudding, sprinkle over the sugar and drizzle over the wine. Return the dish to the oven, covered, for 15-20 minutes or until the plums are soft.

Ginger cake

Prep and cook time: 1 hour 10 minutes
serves: 10-12

Ingredients:
200 g | 7 oz self-raising flour
100 g | 3 ½ oz | ½ cup sugar
1 tbsp ground ginger
1 tsp bicarbonate of soda
50 g | 1 ¾ oz | ½ stick butter
100 g | 3 ½ oz | ⅓ cup golden syrup
45 g | 1 ½ oz marmalade
1 egg
200 ml | 7 fl. oz | ⅞ cup milk

Method:

Heat the oven to 180°C (160° fan) 375F, gas 5. Line a
20 cm x 20 cm / 8" x 8" baking tin with baking parchment.

Put the flour, sugar, ginger and bicarbonate of soda into
a mixing bowl.

Put the butter, golden syrup and marmalade in a pan and
heat gently until just melted. Whisk in the egg with the milk.

Stir the melted butter mixture into the flour, mix until smooth
and pour the mixture into the baking tin. Bake for 40-50 minutes
until golden. Leave the cake to cool in the tin, carefully remove
it and serve with crème fraiche or whipped cream.

Chocolate puddings

Prep and cook time: 35 minutes
serves: 4

Ingredients:
125 g | 4 ½ oz | ½ cup butter
200 g | 7 oz | 1 cup sugar
4 eggs
100 g | 3 ½ oz | ⅔ cup ground almonds
100 g | 3 ½ oz | 1 cup self-raising flour
250 g | 9 oz dark chocolate,
finely chopped
vanilla ice-cream, to serve

Method:

Heat the oven to 180°C (160° fan) 375F, gas 5 and grease 4 small pudding moulds with butter.

Beat the butter and sugar together until fluffy then add the eggs and mix well. Fold in the ground almonds and flour and stir in the chocolate.

Pour the mixture into the moulds and bake in the oven for 18-20 minutes. Test with a wooden toothpick, if it comes out clean, the puddings are done.

Turn out the puddings and serve whilst they are warm with vanilla ice-cream.

Apricot crumble

Prep and cook time: 40 minutes
serves: 4

Ingredients:
200 g | 7 oz | 2 cups plain
(all-purpose) flour
150 g | 5 oz | 2 ½ sticks butter
150 g | 5 oz | ¾ cup brown sugar
75 g | 2 ½ oz | 1 cup flaked
(slivered) almonds
3 tsp cinnamon
800 g | 1 ¾ lbs | 4 cups apricots,
stoned and halved
a small pinch of saffron, dissolved in
boiling water
2 tsp cinnamon

Method:

Heat the oven to 200°C (180° fan) 400F, gas 6.

Place the flour, butter, sugar and 2 teaspoon of cinnamon
in a food processor and pulse until the mixture resembles
breadcrumbs. Mix in the almonds and set aside.

Put the apricots in an ovenproof dish with most of their juice.
Add the saffron and 1 teaspoon of the cinnamon.

Scatter over the crumble topping, sprinkle over the remaining
cinnamon and bake in the oven for 20-25 minutes.

Serve with custard or ice-cream.

Plum muffins

Prep and cook time: 35 minutes
serves: 12

Ingredients:
225 g | 8 oz | 1 cup butter
200 g | 7 oz | ⅞ cup sugar
a pinch of salt
4 eggs
300 g | 11 oz | 3 cups plain
(all-purpose) flour
50 g | 1 ¾ oz | ⅓ cup ground almonds
2 tsp baking powder
600 g | 1 ¼ lbs plums,
stoned and stewed

Method:
Preheat the oven to 200°F (180° fan) 400F, gas 6 and grease a 12 hole muffin tin with butter.

Beat the butter, sugar and salt together until light and fluffy then beat in the eggs one at a time.

Fold in the flour, almonds and baking powder and drop a spoon of the batter into each muffin form, add about a tablespoon of the plums then spoon on the rest of the batter.

Bake the muffins in the oven for 20-25 minutes until golden brown. Test with a wooden toothpick, if it comes out clean, the muffins are done.

Cranberry upside-down cake

Prep and cook time: 1 hour 10 minutes
serves: 8

Ingredients:
3 eggs
150 g | 5 oz | ⅔ cup sugar
1 lemon, zest
150 g | 5 oz | 1 cup plain
(all-purpose) flour
1 tsp baking powder
1 tsp cocoa powder
100 g | 3 ½ oz dark chocolate,
chopped
150 g | 5 oz | ⅔ cup sugar
200 g | 7 oz cranberries

Method:
Heat the oven to 200°C (180° fan), 400F, gas 6. Grease a
20 cm / 8" springform cake tin.

To make the cake mixture, beat the eggs, sugar and lemon
zest together. Sift the flour, baking powder and cocoa powder
into the bowl and stir in the chocolate.

Sprinkle sugar into the cake tin and spread the cranberries
evenly over the base. Pour the cake mixture on top and bake
for 50 minutes.

Remove the cake from the oven and leave it to cool
completely on a wire rack. Upturn the cake onto a plate
and serve with whipped cream or crème fraiche.

Rhubarb semolina pudding

Prep and cook time: 35 minutes
serves: 4

Ingredients:
8 stalks rhubarb, trimmed and chopped
60 g | 2 oz sugar
125 ml | 4 ½ fl. oz | ½ cup white wine
425 g | 15 oz | 2 cups canned semolina
(cream of wheat) pudding
110 g | 4 oz | 1 ½ cups flaked
(slivered) almonds
125 g | 4 ½ oz | 1 cup corn flakes

Method:
Heat the oven to 200°C (180° fan) 400F, gas 6.

Put the chopped rhubarb in an ovenproof dish and
scatter over the sugar. Pour over the wine, cover with foil
and bake in the oven for 15 minutes.

Pour over the semolina pudding, scatter with the almonds and
corn flakes and return to the oven, uncovered, for 10 minutes.

Apple crumble cake

Prep and cook time: 1 hour 15 minutes
serves: 8

Ingredients:
175 g | 6 oz | ¾ cup butter
150 g | 5 oz | ⅔ cup sugar
3 eggs
200 g | 7 oz | 2 cups plain
(all-purpose) flour
2 tsp baking powder
150 g | 5 oz | ¾ cup crème fraiche
4 bramley apples, peeled,
cored and chopped

For the crumble topping:
75 g | 2 ½ oz | ¾ cup flour
75 g | 2 ½ oz | ½ cup ground almonds
30 g | 1 oz brown sugar
1 tsp cinnamon
50 g | 2 oz | ½ stick butter

Method:

Heat the oven to 180°C (160° fan) 375F, gas 5. Grease and line a cake tin about 20 cm / 8" in diameter.

Cream the butter and sugar until light and fluffy. Beat in the eggs one at a time, then add the flour and baking powder.

Fold in the crème fraiche, then mix in the apples and turn the batter into the greased cake tin.

Clean the mixing bowl and add all the ingredients for the crumble topping. Rub them together with your fingertips until the mixture resembles breadcrumbs and scatter the topping over the cake.

Bake in the oven for 35-40 minutes or until golden brown. Test with a wooden toothpick, if it comes out clean, the cake is done.

Rhubarb and strawberry gratin

Prep and cook time: 30 minutes
serves: 4

Ingredients:
25 g | 1 oz | ¼ stick butter, softened
4 sticks rhubarb, chopped
450 g | 1 lb strawberries, halved
60 g | 2 oz sugar
850 g | 1 ¾ lb ready-made custard
icing (confectioners') sugar, to garnish

Method:

Preheat the oven to 180°C (160° fan) 375F, gas 5.

Rub the butter onto the base and sides of an ovenproof dish.

Spread the rhubarb and strawberries into the dish, scatter over the sugar and pour over the custard.

Bake in the oven for 15-20 minutes and serve sprinkled with the icing sugar.

Baked pears in honey

Prep and cook time: 35 minutes
serves: 4

Ingredients:
4 firm pears
200 ml | ⅞ cup sweet white wine
60 ml | 2 fl. oz honey
1-2 tsp cinnamon

Method:

Heat the oven to 180°C (160° fan) 375F, gas 5.

Peel the pears, leaving the stalk intact and slice off the bottoms so they sit evenly. Place in an ovenproof dish.

Pour over the wine, drizzle over the honey and sprinkle over the cinnamon.

Cover with foil, leaving plenty of space for the pears to steam in the liquid, and bake in the oven for 25-30 minutes, basting from time to time, or until the pears are tender.

Serve with ice-cream or crème fraiche.

Chocolate pudding cake

Prep and cook time: 35 minutes
serves: 4-6

Ingredients:
4 eggs
4 egg yolks
200 g | 7 oz | 1 cup caster
(superfine) sugar
200 g | 7 oz | ⅞ cups butter, melted
150 g | 5 oz | 1 ½ cups plain
(all-purpose) flour
50 g | 2 oz | ½ cup cocoa powder
200 g | 7 oz | 1 ⅓ cups chopped
dark (plain) chocolate
icing (confectioners') sugar

Method:
Heat the oven to 200°C (180° fan) 400F, gas 6. Grease a
20 cm x 30 cm / 8" x 12" ovenproof dish.

Beat the eggs and egg yolks together with the sugar until
the mixture is pale and fluffy, then beat in the melted butter.
Fold in the flour, cocoa powder and chopped chocolate
and pour into the dish.

Bake the pudding for 20-25 minutes or until the cake is firm
to the touch. Allow it to cool a little then dust with icing sugar
and serve with whipped cream or ice-cream.

Rhubarb bread pudding

Prep and cook time: 35 minutes
serves: 4

Ingredients:
2 sticks rhubarb, stewed
2 tbsp butter, softened
6 slices white bread
60 g | 2 oz sugar
1 tsp cinnamon
250 ml | 9 fl. oz | 1 cup cream
4 eggs
icing (confectioners') sugar

Method:

Heat the oven to 200°C (180° fan) 400F gas 6. Butter the base and sides of an ovenproof dish.

Arrange the bread neatly in the dish, overlapping the slices, and sprinkle over the sugar and cinnamon.

Whisk the cream with the eggs and pour over the bread.

Place the stewed rhubarb over the top and bake for 20 minutes, until golden brown. Dust with icing sugar before serving.

index

index.

index.